Politics, Economics
and Welfare

Politics, Economics and Welfare

An Elementary Introduction to Social Choice

John Bonner

Senior Lecturer in Economics,
University of Leicester

DISTRIBUTED BY HARVESTER PRESS

First published in Great Britain in 1986 by
WHEATSHEAF BOOKS LTD.
A MEMBER OF THE HARVESTER PRESS PUBLISHING GROUP
Publisher: John Spiers
Director of Publications: Edward Elgar
16 Ship Street, Brighton, Sussex

British Library Cataloguing in Publication Data

Bonner, John
    Politics, economics and welfare: an elementary introduction to
    social choice theory.
    1. Social choice
    I. Title
    302.1'3 Hb846.8

    ISBN 0-7108-0207-2
    ISBN 0-7108-0222-6 Pbk

Typeset in 11/12 Times Roman by Paul Hicks Ltd., Middleton,
Manchester
Printed and bound in Great Britain by
Biddles Ltd., Guildford and King's Lynn

THE HARVESTER PRESS PUBLISHING GROUP
The Harvester Press Publishing Group comprises Harvester Press
Limited (chiefly publishing literature, fiction, philosophy,
psychology, and science and trade books), Harvester Press
Microfilm Publications Limited (publishing in microfilm
unpublished archives, scarce printed sources, and indexes to these
collections) and Wheatsheaf books Limited (a wholly independent
company chiefly publishing in economics, international politics,
sociology and related social sciences), whose books are distributed
by Harvester Press Limited and its agencies throughout the world.

Contents

List of Figures

Preface

The aim of this book is to provide a readable, elementary introduction to the main themes of what has become known as social choice theory. A study of the formal properties of group decision-making procedures, and of their consequences for the meaning and measurement of group rather than individual welfare, ought to have important and interesting lessons for the ordinary citizen as well as for the student of the social sciences. That they are not more widely appreciated is due in part to the highly specialised and mathematical language in which the debate has often been conducted. To translate the results into simple examples, however, is unsatisfactory and unsatisfying. Stripped of the logical argument which precedes them, conclusions can appear strange and unconvincing. So an attempt has been made to explain some of the supporting theory with the aid of little more than basic arithmetic and geometry, first-year economics and several rather silly exercises. What is lost in technical brilliance and precision is intended to be balanced by wider understanding.

As befits an elementary textbook with no claims to originality, all the ideas and many of the illustrations are drawn from superior authorities. Due acknowledgement is given in the references and reading sections at the end of each chapter, rather than interrupt the narrative with every point of indebtedness. (Place, publisher, and dates of books can be found in the bibliography.) But the reader should be warned that simplification is as dangerous as it is tempting. Arguments can be misconstrued or distorted. The search for ease in style and presentation can give the impression that matters are settled when, in fact, they are still subject to major disagreement. Even the omission of terms and definitions familiar to the professional, on the ground that they are not essential to an understanding of the central issue, lays the text open to the criticism that it ignores crucial developments in the literature. It is certainly not a comprehensive guide.

While political science and social philosophy cannot be excluded from any comprehensive discussion of social choice and social welfare, it is the economist's concern with the meaning and measurement of welfare or utility which largely determines the general direction of the book and its selection of set pieces. The words 'welfare' and 'utility' are used interchangeably throughout, while the distinctions between choice and judgement about welfare and between sophisticated and manipulative voting are treated with some reserve. In particular, little or no reference is made to the vast literature on the borders of economics and politics, sometimes called political economy, which has spread from books such as Anthony Downs, *An Economic Theory of Democracy,* J. M. Buchanan and Gordon Tullock, *The Calculus of Consent* and Marcus Olson Jnr., *The Logic of Collective Action.* Perhaps exemplified by the Centre for the study of Public Choice, and its journal *Public Choice,* such literature concentrates on the practical problems of finding decision-making procedures which work, emphasises the importance of rules and constitutions rather than outcomes, and tends to regard the alleged impossibility of social choice as irrelevant. Without denying the progress that has been made by the application of the methods of economics to the problems of politics, or in any way under-valueing the importance of public choice arguments, this book considers the alternative approach still worthy of attention. A proper understanding of social choice should inform the reader's appreciation of public choice. In any case, to do justice to the latter would require another book. So what follows might be described as having an Arrow bias on social choice, a Sen bias on social welfare, and a Samuelson bias on almost everything else.

My colleagues Ian Bradley, Bob Borthwick and Martin Hoskins have kindly read some or all of these chapters in draft and tried, along with various referees, to correct the author's failings in content and design. They should not be blamed for the nonsense that remains. Finally, the author is indebted to Sonia Brewster, Renie Groves and Judith Smith who struggled with his handwriting to produce typewritten versions of first, second and even third attempts.

1 Individual Welfare

The concept of social welfare is frequently used in judgements about the effects of changes in social, political and economic circumstances upon groups of individuals, and as the basis for policy prescriptions to deal with the social, political and economic problems that face these groups. Whether reference is made to the 'interests' or 'satisfactions' of the members of a club, trade union or class, to the 'well-being' of a local community or a whole nation, the notion is much the same: if a change in circumstances or implementation of a policy somehow increases the welfare of the individuals in question, then that change is good and that policy is desirable. These conclusions can be reached without much thought or precision, and the purpose of the next three chapters is to explain the many difficulties involved in describing and measuring social welfare. Ideally, those who make decisions on behalf of groups of individuals should have the welfare of those individuals in mind, and if an unambiguous and publicly acceptable index or measure of social welfare were available then their task would be relatively straightforward and simple. Realistically it is necessary to allow for the fact that people in power may be looking after their own interests rather than those for whom they act, and because welfare can mean so many different things, making unambiguous judgements about the welfare of non-identical individuals is an almost impossible task.

An individual's welfare does not depend solely on material goods and services consumed, however basic they may be to the maintenance of life. The amount of work that has to be performed, adjusted for its pleasantness or unpleasantness, in order to obtain these goods and services is obviously an important additional factor. So too must be the individual's health, family and friends, freedoms and liberties, and even spiritual and psychological attitudes. Indeed the capacity to 'enjoy', 'take pleasure in', 'benefit from' their economic, social and cultural circumstances

1

could make a significant difference to their overall 'happiness'. Moreover it could be argued that an individual's welfare does not depend on circumstances at one point of time but over their lifespan; and an individual with limited endowments now but with excellent prospects for the future and an expectation of a long life is, in a sense, 'well off'.

At least, this is how most people would judge their own and other people's welfare. *Judgement* is the key word. There is no other source of information about welfare, although there may be a description of the things that are judged to affect welfare. Exactly how these judgements are made, how advantage in one direction is balanced or offset by disadvantage in another, how the well-being or sufferings of different individuals can be compared, are the difficult parts of the exercise. There is no doubt that comparisons and evaluations of this kind are commonplace. Yet they do not have to be precise or accurate because they are never put to serious purposes. Statements like 'I feel better off this year than last', or 'I am better off than poor old so and so', or 'He is worse off than lucky you-know-who' are frequently expressed but rarely tested. To give them accuracy and precision requires both a detailed analysis of individual circumstances and a method of measuring them. Only then can questions like, 'how much better off are you compared with last year'? or, 'Is he better off than you-know-who or is she'? can be answered. In other words, the way in which individual welfare is to be measured must be amenable to *interpersonal comparison*.

Suppose a comprehensive description of individual circumstances were available, and suppose further that individuals could be persuaded to mark a 'score-card' for welfare. Against each factor or dimension of welfare, such as 'material goods' or 'health', they were asked to mark themselves, and others, out of a maximum possible score of 10. A zero mark, they would be told, means that in their opinion the individual derives no welfare or satisfaction from a factor or dimension of circumstance; and a mark of 10 means that the individual could not possibly do better. It is important to note that they are not being asked to mark for merit or for what they think people deserve. The

numbers are meant to measure welfare of the actual
conditions of economic, social, cultural and political life,
and not to represent opinions of how these conditions come
about, by the individual's own efforts or by others, by
accident or design, legally or illegally. Given these rules, an
imaginary score-card, for a very simplified list of circumstances, might look something like this:

Individual A's judgement (marks out of 10) of welfare

	For himself	For individual B
Material goods	5	8
Work	5	8
Freedoms	8	8
Health	5	5
Friends and family	8	2
Mental attitudes	8	0

When challenged about his marks, individual A might say
that he is none too happy about his own material goods,
work or health, but he is reasonably happy about his
freedoms, friends and family, and mental attitude. However, he thinks individual B, although better off in terms of
material goods and work, suffers from being miserable all
the time and has few friends and no family.

Now these are perfectly legitimate opinions to hold. The
question is whether the marks or numbers provided can be
used with any confidence to measure welfare. In the first
place they are *subjective,* based on the opinions of individual
A: a subjective judgement of allegedly objective conditions.
There is no reason to believe that individual B, or any other
individual for that matter, would agree with them for either
A or B. It would be nice to believe that subjective
judgements can be avoided. Unhappily as subsequent
arguments will try to show, there are no purely objective
standards of welfare measurement. Secondly, even individual A's marks may not be awarded *consistently.* He may
change his mind every time he is asked to fill up the
score-card, and give different marks for the same individual
circumstances. Alternatively he may think that individual B
gains the same amount of welfare or satisfaction from his
freedom as he does himself, yet award him a different mark.
Too much inconsistency ruins the accuracy and comparabil-

ity of any scheme of measurement.

It also suggests deeper problems involving the *precision* and *discrimination* of the marks. Can individuals distinguish between the intervals of marks between 0 and 10? Can they always be relied upon to give higher marks to those individuals and categories of circumstance which they judge to have or to yield higher welfare? When individual A awards a mark of 8 for individual B's freedoms and 2 for his family and friends, does that mean that A judges B to enjoy exactly twice as much welfare from the former category than from the latter? Do marks of 5 for the same category mean that one individual is judged to enjoy exactly the same amount of welfare as the other? It may well be that individuals feel more confident of their marks about categories such as material goods and work than they do about categories such as mental attitude or health, and more certain of their scoring for their own circumstances than for someone else's.

All this becomes important in the context of the fourth and last problem area when the numbers are used to make judgements about the total welfare of both individuals. Only the relative welfare of each individual from each category or from the point of view of each individual is revealed. As the imaginary score-card stands, can the numbers be added or multiplied together? There is certainly a strong temptation, when faced with two columns of numbers, to add them up and declare individual A the winner with a total of 39 compared to 31 for individual B. While individual A was only asked to score each category out of 10, it would seem logical to assume that he also, implicitly, marked the combined categories out of 60. However, it may be dangerous to push the argument that far because scoring for total welfare might be quite a different sort of exercise. If individual A has been told that he was expected to judge his own individual B's total welfare, and that his marks for each category were to be combined together, he might have produced another score-sheet. He might have argued that the list of factors affecting individual welfare was incomplete, and would have wanted to include one called 'Earning credits in heaven'. Moreover he might have felt that it was more important than all the others, and should be marked out of 20, not 10. Or he might have substituted the more sophisticated criticism that the categories or factors of circumstance do not act independently on individual welfare. Mental attitudes, for example, could affect enjoyment from the consumption of material goods and services, and ill-health could increase the unpleasantness of work. Finally, anyone adding up numbers knows that they can be arrived at in many different ways. The sum of three scores of 8 and three scores of 5 is 39, as in the imaginary example for individual A; but so is the sum of five scores of 7 and one score of 4, and so on through many other combinations. Does it matter? Is each category to be counted equal, to carry the same weight in the overall index of welfare? Is 39 or any other total to represent the same overall welfare level regardless of how it is composed?

With all these doubts and difficulties, further progress towards the measurement of welfare seems doomed to failure. Not only does the chosen method produce as many numbers as there are individuals with different opinions, it is also threatened by having to deal with as many different ways of adding them up. Perhaps the fault lies in the subjective approach. There may be more objective ways of measuring individual welfare. Instead of asking individuals to give their opinions, try instead to observe their circumstances and attach a number in terms of physical units to each factor or category. These physical units could be calorie intake for food consumption, space and availability of clean water for housing, number of pairs of shoes or suits or coats for clothing. Similar attempts after all have been made to determine standards of absolute poverty. Work can be mesasured by hours, adjusted for physical exertion, noise levels or time spent sitting down. Even freedoms, friends and family can be counted.

Unfortunately, some kinds of health (pain) and most aspects of mental capacity evade quantification. Morever, there is no obvious way of putting all the information collected and collated together in a single index of welfare. Do more calories, more space, more friends and less work automatically lead to more welfare? What is the connection between these variables and an individual's welfare? How can calories, living.space, number of friends and freedoms, and all those factors of welfare which can be measured in units of some kind, be added up? Each separate unit may make sense in its own sphere and yet make less sense than subjective marks out of 10 when combined with others. All that can be said is that an individual with more of everything regarded as somehow 'good', has more welfare than an individual with less of everything. It is not at all clear what can be said about an individual with more of some and less of others. Some may not even like more space or more calories, and in the end the need for subjective judgements is no different from and no less exhaustive than that facing the previous score-card marking scheme.

INDIVIDUAL UTILITY

In the search for an objective and unique measure of individual welfare, the greatest progress has been claimed by economists with their notion of utility and of the individual's willingness to pay for utility. Inevitably their index of welfare is less extensive and ambitious, but it retains many of the underlying assumptions of the previous analysis. In particular well-being, happiness, and welfare are to be correlated with the 'good'. Some economic, political and social circumstances are better for individuals because they bring those individuals more welfare. They are not better because they make for a better society, because individuals deserve them, because they more closely satisfy a system of natural law, a moral code, or because they obey the commandments of the Almighty. There is no suggestion that the 'good' might be met by less welfare, self-denial or suffering. By adding the strong presumption that individuals are the best judges of their own welfare, most economists are satisfied by the substitution of the words 'the economic, political and social circumstances most preferred by individuals' for 'the best economic, political and social circumstances'. The concept of the 'good' is evidently hedonistic and individualistic.

This is not the place to rehearse the economist's theory of

demand or of consumer behaviour. Its implications for utility measurement, however, merit careful consideration. A simple approach, associated with an earlier tradition, used utility to denote the satisfaction derived from commodities consumed; that is, what the consumer buys. Utility was supposed to increase as the number of units consumed increased, but the consumer's satisfaction was eventually subject to a law of *diminishing marginal utility*. Utility derived from a commodity (all others held constant) increases at a declining rate: the additions to total utility will eventually start to decline for each (small) additional unit of the commodity. It should be noted that total utility is a function of all units consumed, not just of the additional unit. With a fixed money income and given prices for all commodities and services on offer, the consumer has an allocation problem. As a rational utility-maximiser he will seek to equate the marginal utility of 'pennies' spent in all directions. For example, if a higher marginal utility could be obtained by spending a little more on wine than would be lost by spending a little less on cheese, then the consumer is not obtaining the most utility from the resources at his disposal, and needs to reallocate his spending in favour of wine. Diminishing marginal utility to each commodity ensures that this problem is manageable. Putting the matter in its simplest form, diminishing marginal utility ensures that there is normally a limit to the consumption of each commodity. In the extreme case of a zero price, the commodity would be consumed up to the point at which its marginal utility has fallen to zero: the point of satiation. An alcoholic (imagines that he) enjoys at least a constant marginal utility from bottles of wine, and may spend all his income in this way. At zero price he (imagines he) could never consume enough.

In Figure 1.1 the theory is described for two commodities consumed by one individual. His demand schedule for cheese is the line AC in (a) (drawn as a straight line for convenience) showing the amounts he is prepared to offer for cheese, declining as the number of units on offer increases. At the price OA, he finds cheese too expensive and is not prepared to buy any; when the price falls to zero,

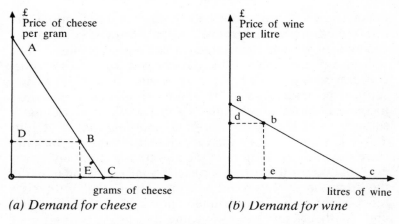

Figure 1.1: Demand schedules and utility measurement

he is satiated with OC; and at the market price OD he is prepared to buy OE units. The same arguments apply to the demand schedule for wine drawn in (b), although the scale of units, the price per unit, and the lengths and distances can be different. One important consequence of having prices and quantities measured, however, is that their products are directly comparable; price × quantity is in the same £ units for wine and cheese. So if the consumer is a utility-maximiser and has solved his allocation problem, and if wine and cheese are the only two commodities he can buy, the £ value of the area OEBD plus the area oebd must equal his total expenditure and, assuming no savings, exhaust his money income.

Where is utility measured? The answer is not directly by any units of its own. Instead, utility is measured indirectly by the amount of his money income the consumer is prepared to give up in exchange for units of cheese or wine. Amounts of utility are inferred from consumer behaviour, from consumer demand, and approximated by amounts of money. When the consumer buys OE units of cheese at market price OD, the utility he derives is reckoned to be much larger than the area OEBD. The correct way of determining the monetary representation of this utility is to ask how much would he pay for the privilege of consuming all the grams between O and OE rather than go without. With a price per unit just below OA, the demand schedule indicates that he would buy his first unit. As the price on offer falls, step by step, the second, third, fourth and fifth units would be bought, and so on down to the OEth unit at OD price. But if the market price is OD per unit, he pays that price for all the units up to the OEth, so he gains a *consumer surplus* on all the rest. The total amount he is prepared to pay is approximated by the area beneath the demand schedule (approximated because the area consists of a number of thin, rectangular columns, with price the height, and 1g the width). He is prepared to pay an amount equal to the £ value of OEBA for OE units, actually pays an amount equal to the £ value of OEBD, and enjoys a consumer surplus equal to the £ value of DBA. It is a measure of the utility he gains by being able to buy cheese at £OD per gram. Depending on scale and prices, it may be smaller or larger in £s than the consumer surplus he enjoys on wine at its current market price (dba).

The utility gains and losses from changes in the availability and-or prices of commodities can now be measured (indirectly) by *changes* in consumer's surplus, provided the consumer's tastes are constant. A fall in the price of wine will lead normally to the purchase of at least one more bottle, and an increase in consumer's surplus on all the rest; a rise in the price of cheese will lead normally to the purchase of at least 1g less, and a fall in the consumer's surplus on all the remaining grams.

Unfortunately, these measurements are in units of money income and move in proportion to utility only so long as the marginal utility of money income remains constant. In other words, the approximation works provided the measuring rod itself does not alter in value. If the consumer's *real income,* the purchasing power of his money income, is also constant there is no problem. But if it increases there is another economist's assumption to undermine confidence in the measuring rod. The marginal utility of real income is set to decline as real income increases: as the consumer feels better off each additional £ of purchasing power will eventually bring smaller and smaller additional units of utility. So even with a constant money income, falling prices could reduce the utility value of £s. Small and isolated movements in the economic circumstances facing the consumer (prices and availability of commodities) may escape the dilemma. When a consumer spends only a small proportion of his income on cheese, a fall in its price, with other prices unchanged, will have little impact on his total real income. It does not follow that the consequent change in utility is insignificant. Added across every consumer who buys cheese, the effects of the price cut could represent a significant increase in the total utility arising from the operations of the cheese industry and still be of little relevance to the total utility of any one individual consumer. By contrast, a poor vegetarian who relies on cheese for most of his protein will feel better off when the price of cheese falls, and be hard hit when its price rises, although the effect may be unimportant for the cheese industry.

An improvement in the real income (purchasing power) of any one individual has to be sought in either an increase in his money income, all prices unchanged, or several price cuts on commodities he buys, money income unchanged, or a single price-cut on a commodity taking a large share of his expenditure, money income unchanged, or some combination of all three. Measuring the contribution of price-cuts to improvements in his real income and utility level would be easier if each commodity could be treated separately and then added together. Even in the case of a single price-cut on the poor vegetarian's cheese, the flexible measuring rod may have to be applied to subsequent effects on his consumption of bread and beans: the utility to be derived from each commodity, that is, may not be independent of the utility derived from the others. In general, some commodities are rival or substitutes in consumption, while some are complements. Wine and cheese might be complements and a fall in the price of cheese could increase the utility derived from spending on wine as well as cheese. Train and plane journeys might be substitutes and a fall in the price of train journeys could reduce spending (and so utility) on plane journeys while it increases the utility derived from spending on train journeys. Combining their effects is no longer a simple matter of adding up separate and independent quantities.

Modern economics still uses the concept of consumer suplus to measure changes in the level of individual utility. *Compensated demand* curves have been introduced to deal with the problem of a fixed-money income and the marginal utility of real income. Along a compensated demand curve a consumer's real income is held constant by adding to money income an amount just sufficient to compensate for a rise in the price of a commodity which takes a significant proportion of total spending, and by subtracting an amount just sufficient to negate the effects of a fall in the price of such a commodity. What remains in the way of changes in demand, normally a rise in demand for a fall in price and a fall in demand for a rise, must be attributable to pure substitution effects. More cheese is bought when its price falls because it is relatively cheap compared to wine, and more wine is bought when the alternative of cheese becomes more expensive, even though the consumer is no better or worse off overall. The area beneath a compensated demand curve, therefore, measures gains or losses in individual utility when constancy in the maginal utility of money income can be assumed. The measuring rod is invariant. But the cost of this progress is that there is no unique compensated demand curve. Each point on the traditional demand curve (e.g. any point between A and C in Fig. 1.1) can represent a different real income level. So each point on the traditional demand curve will then be on its own compensated demand curve. The appropriate compensated demand curve will cut through the traditional and demand curve at each point, downwards from left to right, and falling more steeply. It will be steeper (and below) for lower prices because the consumer will increase consumption by a smaller amount if money income is adjusted downwards.

The consequences for measurement of the effects of changes in individual circumstances, like a fall in the price of one of the commodities the consumer buys, is that there are now *three* alternatives: either the change in the area beneath two points on the traditional demand curve (one for the price before and one for the price after the fall) with the prospect of variations in the measuring rod, or the change in the area beneath the compensated demand curve drawn through the original price, or the change in the area beneath the compensated demand curve drawn through the new lower price. That is, following the details of Figure 1.2 for a fall in price from P_1 to P_2, the new areas P_1CFP_2 (under the compensated demand curve through point C) and P_1EDP_2 (under the compensated demand curve through point D).

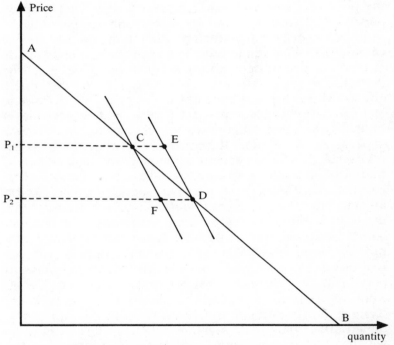

Figure 1.2: Compensated demand curves

The area P_1CFP_2, which is smaller than the traditional measurement of P_1CDP_2, is called the *compensating variation* or the minimum amount of money that needs to be subtracted from the consumer's income to leave the level of utility or enjoyment as it was at C, but with the new lower price. The area P_1EDP_2, which is larger than the traditional measurement, is called the *equivalent variation,* or the minimum amount of money that needs to be added to the consumer's income to keep the level of utility or enjoyment as it is at D, but with the old higher price. They all appear to measure the same thing: how much better off the consumer is as a result of the fall in price. (For a rise in price, and a fall in utility the positions are reversed: the compensating variation becomes the minimum amount to be added to money income so as to restore the original level of utility, and the equivalent variation becomes the minimum amount to be subtracted from money income to maintain level of utility after price change, P_2DEP_1, and P_2FCP_1 respectively.)

Thus the two new measures set upper and lower bounds to the area under the traditional demand curve, and they will only narrow to the same amount when the change caused by the price movement has a small income effect on the commodity's demand, i.e. when the main effects are substitution. Consumer surplus under the traditional demand curve will approximate to a reasonable money measure of such changes in individual utility levels only when this condition is met. Moreover, the connection between the absolute level of an individual's utility—which may be of some relevance—and money income is still remote. Apart from the problem of price changes, it is bound to be an underestimate of the sum of consumer's surpluses he enjoys on all the commodities he buys, and there is no way of making sense of that calculation. There may be some point in asking how much of his income he would be prepared to sacrifice to retain the opportunity of buying a single commodity, but no point in asking him the same question about all the commodities at once. Besides, any analysis of an individual's utility level which ignores his role as a producer is incomplete. Where does his money income come from? Ownership of the factors of production, of personal labour as well as land and capital, is the source of claims on resources for consumption. For most people the sale of labour—the supply of work—is the major source, and their incomes depend on the wages they are paid and the number of hours they work. The ownership of personal labour, from this point of view, is an endowment of leisure.

Leisure and commodities are 'good', work is 'bad' and yields disutility. Its disutility increases with the number of hours of leisure lost. So wages have to overcome the disutility, and each individual worker has a supply schedule relating the number of hours of work to the hourly wage, which increases as the total number of hours worked increases. He supplies labour up to the point at which the additional disutility from the additional (marginal) hour of work equals the going hourly wage rate. From the fact that all hours worked earn the same wage, it can be deduced that the worker enjoys a *producer's surplus* analagous to his consumer's surplus on commodity markets. The surplus is the difference between what he actually earns and the lowest amount he would have accepted for supplying all those hours.

Trying to find an unambiguous monetary representation of producer's surplus is even more difficult and treacherous than it was in the case of consumer's surplus, and no attempt will be made here to follow the argument. For present purposes it is enough to recognise them as two sides of the welfare the individual gains from his economic activities. Neither is wholly independent of the other. While a rise in wage-rates makes him better off through his producer's surplus, he does not have to take the improvement in the form of higher income. There is a tendency to treat the purpose of the whole exercise as one of obtaining claims in resources for consumption, now and in the future, and to forget the utility derived from leisure. If higher income is taken then its value will depend on the price he pays in commodity markets, on his consumer's surplus position. But he may be content to take more leisure hours. Alternatively, if he is forced to work harder or in more unpleasant conditions for the same money income, and commodity prices remain as before, he will feel worse off through a loss in producer's surplus which has no counterpart in consumer's surplus. Once again, amounts of money income are a poor reflection of changes in his overall utility.

The modern theory of consumer behaviour, like the older theory of demand and utility, is best explained with the use of simple diagrams. In Figure 1.3 consumer choice between commodities is illustrated in (a) and worker choice between income and leisure in (b). Unfettered choice is one of the most important assumptions of the model. On the side of commodities, the consumer is given a budget, or an endowment in terms of total claims on wine and cheese. He can have either OA units of cheese (and no wine), or OB units of wine (and no cheese), or one of the different combinations of cheese and wine along the line joining A and B. The slope of the line is determined by the relative

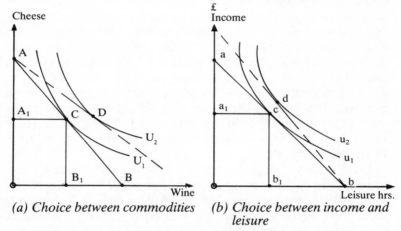

(a) *Choice between commodities*   (b) *Choice between income and leisure*

Figure 1.3: Indifference curves and utility measurement

price of cheese and wine. If the slope were 1:1 then 1 unit of cheese could always be exchanged for 1 unit of wine; if 1:½ then 1 unit of cheese would 'cost' only ½ unit of wine, or 1 unit of wine would cost 2 units of cheese, and so on. The consumer is allowed to choose his best (most preferred) combination along AB. The budget line is the only constraint under which he operates. What he maximises no longer has to be called 'utility', maximising just means making the best use of his claims on consumption resources. He chooses combination C, with OA_1 units of cheese an OB_1 units of wine. Why combination C? One explanation is to imagine the space between the axes of the figure to be like a hill of 'pleasure'. Its peak is somewhere out to the north-east, in the opposite direction from the origin of the figure, which is naturally the lowest point. Contours of 'pleasure' can be drawn to indicate the general shape of the hill: it rises from the two axes as well as from the origin. Two such contours are given and labelled U_1 and U_2. They are lines joining combinations of cheese and wine which give equal pleasure, in much the same way as contours of height are drawn on geographers' maps, and denoted by economists as 'indifference curves'. The consumer is supposed to be indifferent between the combinations on each curve because they give the same pleasure. Now it can be seen why the consumer chooses point C. It enables him to get as far up the hill of pleasure as his claims on wine and cheese, and their relative prices, permit. He can only climb higher up the hill, to a point such as D, by either having his total claims on resources increased (represented by a parallel outward shift in the budget line AB, more cheese and wine) or having the price of (one of) the commodities cut (illustrated by the budget line tilting through A to form the dotted line AD, and representing a fall in the relative price of wine).

Diminishing marginal utility with respect to each commodity has disappeared, only to be partially replaced by *diminishing marginal rates of substitution* between commodities. To imagine the consumer moving around the hill of pleasure along one on the contours, is to put him in the position of substituting one commodity for the other, cheese for wine or wine for cheese, so as to keep his level of pleasure or preference constant. Were additional units of the two commodities always of the same pleasure or preference to him, regardless of how many units he already enjoyed, then the contours would be straight lines.

In Figure 1.4 cheese is measured in grams and wine in centilitres. Combinations of cheese and wine are described by putting the number of grams first and the number of centilitres second. Along indifference 'curve' U* the consumer obtains equal pleasure from (0, 6), (3, 3), and (6, 0). To maintain equal pleasure, in other words, he always has to substitute 1 additional cl of wine for the loss of 1 gm of cheese. Because the straight line indifference 'curve' is drawn to touch both axes, he can also manage without any

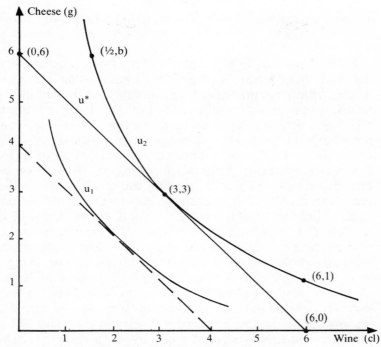

Figure 1.4: Diminishing marginal rates of substitution

wine or cheese provided he has enough of the other commodity. Technically, he has a constant marginal rate of subsitution between commodities. A normal shaped indifference curve drawn through the point (3, 3) shies away from both axes, indicating that as the consumer posseses more and more of one commodity (and less and less of the other) he requires larger and larger additional units to compensate him for the further loss of one (small) unit of the other. Close to the point (3, 3) to 1 g of cheese compensates for the loss of 1 cl of wine, but close to the point (1½, 6) the ratio is more like 5 g of cheese for 1 cl of wine; and moving in the other direction from (3,3) to (6,1), the ratio goes from 1 cl of wine compensating 1g of cheese to something like 6 cl of wine needed to compensate for the loss of 1 g of cheese. The more cheese the consumer has the lower is its value in terms of wine; the more wine the consumer has the lower is its value in terms of cheese. His marginal rate of substitution declines in both commodities, although not necessarily at the same rate.

From these simple beginnings the previous conclusions of demand theory can be reached without using the word utility, or any commitment to monetary measures of utility. Indifference curves are labelled to indicate that one is above another; but even the word pleasure can be removed, and the labelling reflects an expression of the consumer's relative preferences. Each indifference curve becomes a border between combinations of cheese and wine which are less preferred (those below and to the left) and combinations which are more preferred (those above and to the right). In particular, the labelling U_1 and U_2 need only indicate that U_2 is preferred to U_1, not by how much U_2 is preferred to U_1.

Identical procedures apply to Figure 1.3(b) depicting the worker's choice between income and leisure. The 'budget' line ab is determined by an initial endowment of leisure hours (ob) and the market wage (slope of ba). With no work done the worker would have zero income. He can choose to be anywhere on the line ab as a maximiser. The hill of pleasure has similar shaped contours, with the peak being out to the north-east: more leisure and/or income are preferred to less. Point c is chosen, with ob_1 leisure hours *remaining* and b_1b hours of work done; income is $£oa_1$. It is the highest point on the hill that the worker can reach given his 'budget'. Points like d can be reached either by an increase in available leisure hours with the wage rate staying unchanged (represented by a parallel outward shift in this line ab), or by a rise in the wage rate with the initial endowment of leisure remaining constant (illustrated by the line ab tilting through b to become the dotted line bd).

The indifference curves labelled U_1 and U_2 need only indicate that combinations of income and leisure on U_2 are preferred to those on U_1. Neither of the two sets of indifference curves have any necessary connection with each other: U_1 and U_2 in commodity space do *not* have to represent the same levels of preference or pleasure as U_1 and U_2 in income and leisure space. Only if the same individual climbs up both hills, or climbs up one without falling down the other, will his overall position warrant the description of an improvement. Rising in one and falling in the other offers no clear evidence. Such a conflict has to be resolved with measures which *quantify* gains and losses so that they can be *added* together; precisely the kind of measurement which has been ruled out.

The formal structure of indifference curves does not preclude other interpretations. Utility could be represented on an indifference map in exactly the same way as height is represented on a contour map. Equal intervals of utility between indifference curves would enable the gradient of the hill of pleasure to be measured, as well as the level of every combination of commodities, or of income and leisure. In this case utility would be measured in units of its own (usually called utils), and an origin (sea level) and a scale required. Monetary measurement of willingness to pay would no longer be used as proxies for utility. The procedure would have more in common with the arbitrary nature of the marking schemes of the first section of this chapter than with the economist's theory of demand. Alternatively, the vertical axis in Figure 1.4 could measure quantities of all commodities other than wine. Movement up and down would then approximate to changes in real income, and the compensation and equivalent variations become the vertical distances between indifference curves, or the utility leads they represented. As with consumer surplus measures, however, no unique answer would emerge unless it could be assumed that the income effect of changes of the price of wine was insignificant.

CARDINAL AND ORDINAL MEASUREMENT

Measurement means attaching numbers to things. Everyone is familiar with the numbers of things like height, weight, temperature, money and performance in examinations or sports events. But the kind of information they provide is very different. Although they all admit qualitative judgements—metres between what is higher and lower, degrees Celsius or Fahrenheit between what is hotter and colder, placings in a race between quicker and slower athletes—they cannot all support the same quantitative manipulation and comparison. It is a matter of origin and scale as well as of units. A simple ranking of athletes in a race reveals little about their relative performance; supplemented with their times it enables judgements to be made about how close they came to winning (or losing), and how much they improved on (or fell short of) their previous best performance. The origin or zero of a scale for measuring height or money is obvious, that for measuring temperature is not. Measuring in metres can be transformed into feet and inches, £s into $s, by direct multiplication or division, leaving relative sizes unaffected. A man who is twice the height of his son in metres will be twice the height of his son in feet; a man who is half as rich as his retired uncle in £s will be half as rich as his retired uncle in $s (ignoring differences in purchasing power). But a town which has twice the average summer temperature of Reykjavik in degrees Celsius will have much less than twice the average summer temperature of Reykjavik in degrees Fahrenheit. Because the two scales have different origins, the transformation between them is more complicated ($F° = 32 + 9/5C°$); and while changes in each (hotter or cooler) will move in the same direction, they will not move in the same proportion.

Measurement systems fall into two broad groups: ordinal and cardinal. Utility measurement which is confined to statements of the form that someone is better or worse off, and not by how much better or worse off they are, remains ordinal even when numbers are used to label the rankings.

Consider the following example of numbers which describe the ranking of an individual's utility levels in four alternative economic circumstances (w, x, y and z):

	Numbers used in ordinal measurement		
w	1	15	32
x	2	16	64
y	3	17	192
z	4	18	384

It does not matter whether the higher or lower number represents the better alternative. All the columns will rank the alternatives in an identical order: either wxyz in descending or ascending order. Neither the absolute nor the relative size of the numbers is of any significance. Assuming that they indicate ascending order, the fact that the number for x in the last column is twice the number for w does not mean that x has twice the utility of w; nor can it be concluded, by similar reasoning, that y has six times the utility of w. Apart from their rankings, the numbers are redundant. Each column simply repeats the ordering of the alternatives, in a *monotonic transformation* of the others: nothing changes, there is no scale or origin, they do not have to be 'converted' by a formula into each other. So symbols could be used instead, or letters of the alphabet, or even the device of writing the alternatives above or below each other to indicate a ranking. Any impression that the use of numbers—and there are countless combinations available—might give of exactness or precision in the measurement of ordinal utility is spurious. The indifference curves of the previous section, U_1 and U_2, were purely ordinal.

By contrast, cardinal measurements do have an origin and a scale, and can provide information about relative sizes. In the next example, the alternatives are ranked in three columns of numbers labelled A, B and C.

Numbers used in cardinal measurement

	A	differences		B	differences		C	differences	
w	0			0			10		
		+2			+10			+4	
x	2		0	10		0	14		0
		+2			+10			+4	
y	4		−1	20		−5	18		−2
		+1			+5			+2	
z	5			25			20		

Let it be assumed to start with that all the numbers are of utility units (utils). Difficult questions about where they have come from can be postponed until their interrelationships have been explored. They are monotomic transformations of each other because they preserve the rankings of w, x, y and z. They are now also *linear transformations* of each other because they are derived by multiplying or

dividing by a constant, or by adding a constant, so that:
   B=5 (A)
   C=10 + 2 (A).
Consequently the signs + or − of the first and second differences between the numbers in each column do not alter, which means that changes in the level of utility, and the rates of change in those levels, always move in the same direction (up or down, faster or slower) between w, x, y and z, whatever set of numbers is being used. In fact, utility levels rise from w through to z at a constant rate from w through to y, and then at a slower rate from y to z.

   Closer inspection shows that columns A and B have even more in common. They are linear transformations on a *ratio scale*. Just like measurement of height in feet or metres, the scales have a common origin and conversion preserves not only the signs of the first and second differences but also their proportions. There is zero utility at w, a doubling of utility between x and y, and a 25 per cent increase between y and z. Column C is only a linear transformation of the others on an *interval* scale. There is no common origin, and although the changes in the utility levels have the right signs, their absolute sizes and proportions are quite different. Utility in column C rises by less than 30 per cent between x and y, and by barely 11 per cent between y and z. It is just like the measurement of temperature on the Celsius and Fahrenheit scales.

   Where might the numbers come from, and how should they be used? One obvious source is the individual himself. He could represent the utility to him of living under the economic circumstances of w, x, y and z on a number scale. If he were capable merely of distinguishing alternatives which gave him more utility from those which gave him less, then the numbers would be as in the first example, an ascending order of preference and offering only ordinal measurement. If he could distinguish the relative strength of his preferences, and describe how the differences in the utility levels of some alternatives were greater than the differences between others, then his numbers would be as in column C, offering cardinal measurement on an interval scale. Finally, if he really could tell by how many times the utility level of the more preferred alternative exceeded that of the less preferred, then the numbers would be as in columns A and B, offering cardinal measurement on a ratio scale. A second source is the judgements of an independent observer, or a committee of economists. They have to invent numbers to describe the utility levels enjoyed by the individual under the four alternatives, irrespective of their own feelings or opinions. While distance may lend objectivity, there is no reason to expect that the external observers will find discriminating between his utility levels any easier. They may have available a wide range of statistics about his circumstance, including his income, upon which to base their judgements, but they still have the problem of converting this information into utility numbers. Even supposing they agree upon some numerical index to describe his alternative circumstances—perhaps £000s worth of resources—they have to decide how many of these £s represent the basic minimum utility level, whether twice as many £s represents less than twice as much utility, and by how much less. They have to invent a transformation formula, which will in turn determine the degree of cardinality in their utility numbers. Applied economics is in exactly this position. The economist's original theory of demand implied measurement on a ratio scale for marginal changes in utility.

The difference between ordinal and cardinal measurement is important because of its implications for *addition*. Cardinal measurement on either ratio or interval scales is acceptable because in most cases only the *differences* in levels of utility are important, whether the addition is across commodities or individuals, whereas ordinal comparisons between the utility gained from cheese and wine, train and plane journeys, can only be combined in terms of direction not amount. If wine and cheese are the only commodities and the individual enjoys more utility from both wine and cheese, or more from wine and no less from cheese, or more from cheese and no less from wine, and they are independent, then the sum of his utility has increased. But nothing can be said about by how much, and nothing can be said about changes in which the utility from cheese rises and that wine falls. The balancing of more or less, the addition of pluses and minuses, requires a cardinal scale. As between individuals, only *levels* of utility can be *compared*.

REFERENCES AND READING

For the application of scaling devices like marking schemes, there is a useful collection of essays edited by Gary M. Maranell, *Scaling: A Source Book for Behavioural Scientists*.

Utility and its measurement is best approached with the aid of one of the leading texts, e.g. P. A. Samuelson, *Economics*, or W. J. Baumol, *Economic Theory and Operations Analysis*.

Utility Theory: A Book of Readings, ed. Alfred N. Page contains several relevant articles and extracts from authorities, past and present. Alfred Marshal, *Principles of Economics*, is still worth reading, in particular Appendix K and the appropriate notes in his 'Mathematical appendix'. A. A. Alchian, 'The meaning of utility measurement', *American Economics Review* (1953) is both wide-ranging and helpful.

The debate between economists about utility and consumer surplus can be followed in Alfred Page (op.cit) but needs to be supplemented by papers collected in Kenneth J. Arrow and Tilbor Scitovsky eds, *Readings in Welfare Economics*, J. R. Hicks, *Wealth and Welfare*, and D. H. Robertson, *Utility and all That*.

I. M. D. Little, *A Critique of Welfare Economics* and P. A. Samuelson *Foundations of Economic Analysis*, offer further debate. Robert D. Willig, 'Consumer surplus without apology' *American Economic Review* (1976) is an important landmark in the modern approach (including his rejoinder in the *American Economic Review* (1979). For an up-to-date survey of the modern literature see Robin Boadway and Neil Bruce, *Welfare Economics*.

2 Social Welfare

It would be nice to think that if all the obstacles in the way of measuring individual welfare were removed or circumvented, the transition to social welfare could be achieved by simple aggregation. Unhapppily not until the transition to social welfare is attempted do all the weaknesses in the concepts of individual welfare become fully apparent. They then serve to compound and confound the search for an acceptable measure of the well-being or collective interest of the group or commumity. Four major questions have to be answered. In the first place the nature and extent of the group of community must be determined: whose welfare is being measured? Secondly, there is the question of whether or not the welfare of the group differs from or is greater than some product of the welfare of the individuals who make up the group. Thirdly, the impact of changes in the distributions of welfare between individuals on total welfare must be assessed. Finally, a decision has to be made about the actual method of arriving at a judgement on social welfare, or how to aggregate social welfare. The issues are interrelated, in that the resolution of one imposes constraints on the resolution of others. Any exclusion of individuals from membership of the group, for example, will obviously restrict assessments of the impact of changes in distribution, and any decision in favour of strongly democratic choice procedures will rule out the addition of many supra-individual elements to social welfare. Of greater significance is the fact that they all assume a notion of individual welfare susceptible to measurement and aggregation in some form. Only a very extreme (and untenable) version of collectivism could ignore altogether the interest, values or needs of individuals in defining social welfare.

So much for what is to come in the rest of this chapter. Whilst the problems of defining and measuring social welfare are being examined, however, there is a danger that the point of the whole exercise will be forgotten. In what

context should social welfare be set? For what purposes is
the concept required? The family is a useful place to start.
Clearly its members are concerned about their own welfare.
They may have some firm ideas about what unites them and
about how one member's welfare depends upon the actions
of others. Senior members may make sacrifices for junior
members. Their opinions and judgements about family
welfare are usually followed by policies designed to improve
the conditions upon which that welfare is based: to move
house, to change jobs, to go on holiday, or to spend the
family budget in a different way. Judgements and the actions
may be confined to the adult members, or even to one adult
member, but they are supposed to be in the interest of the
whole family. When all the members are allowed to
contribute to both judgements and actions, debate, discussion, argument or threat may precede the outcome. Clashes
of individual interests have to be reconciled and cooperation
between individuals somehow encouraged. An informal
mechanism for reaching decisions that affect the whole
family will have to be developed; whether it will be
dictatorial or more like a committee agreeing to abide by
majority rule does not matter for the moment.

Yet there is quite a different context in which the welfare
of the family may be judged, and that is by an independent
observer. The independent observer need not consult any
member of the family, nor agree with them when they are
consulted. The observer's conclusions are supposed to be
reached after an objective and balanced assessment of the
family's circumstances. They are not the product of idle
curiosity, but the necessary preliminary to benevolent
policy-making. The social scientist, the civil servant, even
the benevolent despot himself, is trying to find the best way
of helping the family to improve its welfare. In varying
degrees they all presume to know more about family welfare
than the family knows itself. At one level the independent
observer may simply attempt to advise the family as to what
it should do to improve its welfare, by consultation and
encouragement rather than by dictation. An another level
he may be part of a long process of official inquiry that ends
in policy being imposed on the family.

What is true for the family may be applied, with amendment, to clubs, trade unions, or whole communities and states. Size may complicate the issue, but not negate the usefulness of the example. Every group must employ a method, or combination of methods, to reach decisions about its welfare. Their social choice procedure may relate to every aspect of economic, political and social life, or they may apply a different procedure to each aspect. It is usual, for example, to think of voting mechanisms for political decisions and the market for economic decisions. Voting mechanisms do not necessarily involve every member of the group. Decisions may be made by a small sub-set of the members, voting democratically among themselves. Even when all members are involved there is no guarantee that their opinions and demands will be counted equally. Whereas most voting procedures are governed by explicit and agreed rules, the market seems to have developed in an informal and haphazard manner and is supposed to rely heavily on self-regulation for its success. Naturally procedures effective in the family or tennis club will be inapplicable to a national trade union or state government. The role of the external observer, however, becomes even more crucial at the national level. Professional social scientists, as modern independent observers, are called upon to give advice and make judgements about national welfare. In doing so they can argue that social science comes into its own with groups rather than individuals, that its study of individuals is incidental to an understanding of human relationships in society, and that its important conclusions are about society as a whole. On one side they are encouraged by the statistical tendency for much individual variety to cancel out when added together, and on the other by the often insistent demands for policy prescriptions to deal with the nation's problems from governments and political parties. Although they will try to support their conclusions with as much 'objective' evidence as possible, there is a strong temptation to assume that social welfare is best considered from outside, that participating individuals do not always know—cannot always know—what is good for the whole, and to introduce their own value-judgements.

They may be right. None the less, the fact that decisions about social welfare are reached by paternalism as well as by social choice based on individual preferences should be remembered. The distinction is somewhat blurred because social scientists have a place in the debate about alternative social choice mechanisms. Advice to governments on how to discover the desires and needs of their citizens, to legislatures on how to conduct their proceedings, and to voters on how to assess policies and programmes, can be valuable without implying any superior knowledge of social welfare and how it is to be measured.

WHOSE WELFARE?

The obvious answer is every member of society: man woman and child. Regrettably human societies can be very exclusive. Membership may be limited to those who are fully paid up, or whose parents were born in the same group, or who belong to the same race. Children may only be admitted as associate members, lacking full rights until they reach the prescribed minimum age. It is interesting to note the difference between the notions of membership implied in the two approaches to judgement about social welfare. Paternalistic approaches tend to include everyone, adults and children, in their judgements, whilst the procedures designed to allow society to reach its own judgements tend to confine responsible and countable opinion to adults. Children are held unfit to engage in such serious decision-making and the parents act on their behalf. So conclusions in this matter, as in so many others relating to social welfare, could depend on whether the values (prejudices) of the members of the group are held to be, separately or collectively, inferior to the values (prejudices) of the independent observer.

One category of membership has so far been ignored. Social welfare is surely a function, in part, of the circumstances of future members of the group or community. Decisions taken by or on behalf of the group now will inevitably have effects which last beyond the life of present members. Individuals may differ very widely in the extent to which they worry about and make provision for the future, whether their own or other people's. Some families may deny themselves in order to benefit children and even grandchildren. Some may spend as if there were no tomorrow. But neither individuals, families nor communities can escape from the transfer of intended and unintended burdens and benefits through time. The consequence (good or bad) of decisions in the past are visited on the present generation, and in turn their acts will add or subtract to the cumulative effect to be passed on to the next. Even those who make provision only for their own future, within their expected lifetime, can be run over by a bus before being able to reap all the returns on their thrift, and so make an unexpected bequest to the next generation. As with individuals and families, so with groups and communities: tennis club committees can plan ahead by securing the ownership of the land on which its courts are built, or go for the short-term advantage and risk the lease running out; governments can protect the environment, preserve the long-term fertility of the soil and slow down the rate of exploitation of scarce mineral resources, or they can allow them to waste away.

Whilst none of these factors can be denied an impact on social welfare, it is far from clear exactly how much of an impact they should be allowed. In terms of sheer numbers there are many more members of society yet to be born than there are existing members. If each of these future members is to be counted of equal worth, then the welfare of existing members would become a small factor in the total. Minimum consumption today/maximum saving for tomorrow, would become the policy conclusion for maximising social welfare (crude addition) over time. By a similar argument the correct conservation policy would be to hand over to the next generation a practically unimpaired supply of scarce natural resources: implying a zero rate of current exploitation. No one—save possibly a very malevolent dictator—would find such extreme conclusions acceptable. When spelt out this way, most people would reject the assumptions upon which they had been built. So looking

after the welfare of future generations is a matter of degree
and balance, a nice calculation of the relative weights to be
placed on their interests compared with those of the present
generation. Probably the future should carry a lower weight
than the present, but to what extent and whether in
proportion to its distance in time from the present remain
the really difficult questions to answer. Moreover the
underlying problem of social welfare surfaces with particular
relevance: *whose* weights are to be applied? Every individual member of society could have a different view about
future generations. How can these divergent weights be
combined, or reconciled, or added up to form the social
view? There is more doubt and uncertainly attached to this
aspect of social welfare than any other, and the next few
chapters will adopt the usual if cowardly expedient of
assuming the problems of time away.

IS THE WHOLE GREATER THAN THE SUM OF THE PARTS?

If social welfare is of an entirely different nature from that of
individual welfare, is affected in quite different ways by the
social, economic and cultural circumstances acting on
individual welfare, and cannot be explained, even in part, by
the sharing of a common characteristic with individual
welfare, then the whole is not the sum of the parts. Indeed it
need not have anything to do with the parts, and social
welfare could move independently from the separate welfares of members of society, even in direct opposition to all
their welfares. If such an extreme position is rejected, the
real issue becomes one of asking, given that the whole has
some relation to the part, are there any ingredients in social
welfare which would make the result different from a crude
sum of individual welfares? It is not so much the way in
which individual welfares are combined as a matter of
whether the group, society or the state has interests which,
in part, override, alter or supplement those of its members.
  The truism that man is a social animal and is everywhere
engaged in activities that depend upon the reciprocity and

cooperation of others—voluntary or forced, conscious or unconscious—suggests the direction in which these additional ingredients might be found. There will be an appeal to the interests of a wider community beyond the individual or the sectional groups to which the individual belongs: from the family to the interests of the state, from local jurisdictions to national interests, from national states to the interests of the world. At each stage the argument will be that the narrow view must be extended to allow for the interrelationships between the 'parts' to encourage individual and sectional activities which benefit the wider community and to restrain or avoid activities which harm it. Only the 'higher' authority is supposed to have the knowledge to interpret the 'wider' interest and the power to control the pursuit of sectional interests.

A similar argument can be introduced from the problems of future generations touched on in the preceding section of this chapter. Individuals and sectional groups may make provision for their own children and grandchildren but are unable to comprehend or predict the mutual repercussions of their decisions on the future for everyone's children and grandchildren. Future generations as a 'whole' may suffer from inadequate investment in new resources or from over-exhaustion of existing resources. Again, only the 'wider' authority is supposed to be able to judge the interests of the future 'whole'.

Both arguments seem to be related to an area of interdependence which the economist calls *externalities*. Individuals may impose costs (or confer benefits) on each other in the normal way of pursuing their own economic interests, which are not balanced by the payment of compensation (or the receipt of income). Actions which others may wish to discourage if imposing costs, or encourage if conferring benefits, are thus not subject to the normal economic incentives. There is a joint, common or collective interest which is not being satisfied. The market system or decentralised, competitive and self-interested decision-making—about which more will be said in Chapter 7—looks as if it has failed to produce the goods. Some kind of public or collective intervention might become justified.

Familiar examples of externalities, such as smokey factory chimneys which pollute the atmosphere, or insect-spraying which protects neighbours from debilitating disease, do seem to share something of the nature of self-defeating arms races between states (as an example of the wider community argument) and the destruction of the long-term natural asset represented by soil fertility (as an example of the future generations argument). Acts which increase individual or sectional welfare can damage social welfare, whilst others may increase social welfare by more than they increase individual or sectional welfare. The additional ingredients in social welfare are a function of the interrelationships between individual welfares. They are not something apart from, of another nature to individual welfare.

DISTRIBUTION

It is possible to ignore altogether the way in which welfare is distributed between members of a group or society, and concentrate instead on aggregate welfare and how the aggregate grows over time. But doing so involves making some very strong value-judgements—implicitly if not explicitly—about the nature of the welfare of the group or society. If distribution is ignored, aggregate welfare does begin to lose its connection with the individual parts; and even a sharp shift in the distribution of a given total of welfare from almost complete equality to extreme inequality would leave the value unchanged. A more acceptable approach is to allow for changes in distribution when adding up individual welfares, to weight the total by the degree of inequality. But now the problem becomes one of finding the appropriate measure of inequality, and defining the value-judgements which can distinguish between welfare values of each degree of inequality. Exactly how much difference to social welfare does a given change in distribution make? Can gains in aggregate welfare be balanced against what are judged to be losses in distributional welfare? Is distance between the lowest and highest level of welfare more important than the absolute level of the poorest individual? Are numbers of more significance than distance; or large numbers of relatively poor members of society worse than a small number very poor? Where are these judgements to be found?

Judgements about distribution are supposed to be impersonal or neutral. It matters that there are rich and poor, not *who* is poor and *who* is rich. Justice or equity requires there be no discrimination between members of society according to their race, religion, sex or colour of hair. Unless, that is, distribution is seen as a reward or punishment for being Protestant, white, male or red-haired, or for the possession of some other personal characteristic. What individuals enjoy in levels of welfare would then be assessed by a standard of personal desert. Such an assessment is not so far fetched as it might seem. Individual welfare cannot be measured directly. Material or economic welfare depends on the claims on resources that the individual inherits, plus the claims he can earn. Even those with the same (lack of) inheritance can earn very different amounts of income. Earnings will depend upon their abilities, the wage-rate and their capacity or willingness to work. The first two factors will be related; those with innate or acquired skills in demand by society will be able to charge high prices for their labour. Willingness to work, however, is a personal, psychological characteristic, reducible in the extreme case to the difference between a lazy and an active person. With everything else being held constant (inheritance, abilities and wage-rates) high income, as a proxy for large amounts of individual welfare, becomes the reward for hard work. Alternatively, what individuals eventually earn or spend may not be thought of as the central issue of equity or justice. Provided everything is done to correct unacceptable inequalities in initial endowments by laws (and taxes) of inheritance, and provided everyone has reasonable access to opportunities of acquiring skills, by education for example, individuals should be left to make their own decisions between work and leisure, and the resulting distribution of income accepted as just. Freedom of choice takes precedence over any notion of equality in terms of final distribution.

Individual members of society will often have conflicting

views about distribution, strongly coloured by their particular position on the spectrum of welfare levels. The poor may be jealous or envious of the rich, and the rich fearful or guilty about the poor. Trying to base social judgements about distribution on individual views or opinions might then appear rather unproductive. The majority (the poor) will always vote for taxing the minority (the rich), at least until the opportunities for benefiting from redistribution run out. There does not seem to be any basis for agreement or consensus on the 'best' or 'better', or even the 'least offensive' distribution. But perhaps too narrow and pessimistic an approach has been taken to individual judgements. Perhaps individuals are capable of taking into account the social consequences of inequalities. Perhaps the rich may vote for some redistribution because they find existing inequalities dangerous. Perhaps the poor will call a halt to redistribution because they begin to worry about its effects on total output. Social welfare is, after all, a function of total welfare *and* distribution, not just distribution. There is some balance to be maintained between the objectives of equity and efficiency. So short-term personal advantage may be overridden by caution and concern about the possible ultimately damaging repercussions of the people's actions. An even stronger support for the possibility of reaching agreement about distribution could be found if individuals were capable of placing themselves in the position of others, in social empathy. The rich may be very happy about distribution as it is, but when confronted with the actual circumstances of the poor may judge them to be morally offensive. They would not like to live in those circumstances, grant that it is wrong to expect anyone else to live in them, and agree to redistribute until the situation of the poorest is improved. The rich would be making the assessment, of course, from their own relative position; the poor might still have another opinion, namely that the redistribution should go much further. It is the difficulty of fully and honestly indentifying with someone else which lies at the root of the problem. One very ambitious method of trying to persuade individuals to make social as distinct from private judgements about distribution is to place them in an imaginary but completely neutral vantage point. Individuals are asked to judge alternative distributions—comprehensive descriptions of the different patterns of circumstances for every member of a group or society—without knowing which particular slot or identity they would occupy. To be precise, they are asked to judge on the basis of an equal chance of occupying any one of the indentities in each distribution. Objectivity and social awareness would come from the realisation that they might just as easily be lucky as unlucky, rich as poor, end up at the bottom as at the top of any distribution. If it were possible to persuade individuals to make imaginative leaps of this kind, they might reach agreement on what is the 'best', or 'least unpleasant' of the alternatives presented. Chapter 9 explores these matters in more detail.

AGGREGATION

Because there is no general agreement about the way in which the basic components of social welfare can be measured, there will be no single set of rules governing its addition. Some will be very precise and others quite vague.

To start, let it be assumed that individual welfare can be directly represented by units unique up to a linear transformation. Let it be further assumed that a description of the circumstances affecting the welfare of every member of the group or society is available for a number of alternative environments: these environments might represent the group or society in different time periods, or before and after some major change in economic, social or cultural conditions. So for each environment—to be called a *social state*—there will be numbers representing the welfare level of every individual.

Imaginary examples for a group consisting of five individuals facing four alternative social states are set out below, and are used as illustrations of the dangers and ambiguities of simple aggregation:

Examples for social welfare aggregation

	Social states			
	w	x	y	z
Individual				
A	500	900	550	550
B	550	900	—	550
C	650	900	700	650
D	800	900	900	850
E	2000	900	2500	2500
Social welfare:	4500	4500	4650	5100

Social state w can be thought of as the original or existing set of circumstances, and comparison made with the other three. With information of this kind, social state w looks as if it provides the same amount of social welfare as x, 150 units less than y, and 600 units less than z. The group should want to move to z as quickly as possible.

Clearly no conclusions along these lines are justified. Ignoring the problem of individual welfare measurement, there is still one of group membership and of interrelationships between members, and of changes in distribution. Assuming that A, B, C, D and E are the only individuals whose welfare is to count, and are all full members, what is the consequence of B's disappearance in social state y? Whether he has died, been expelled, or is deemed to have no more importance in calculations of social welfare, does that fact not undermine any comparison made between y and the other social states? Putting the matter very crudely, are another 150 units of social welfare between w and y worth the extinction of B? Equally important is the need to be sure that the numbers in each column take into account all aspects of individual welfare, including interdependence. The 550 units recorded for individual B in social state w, for instance, might not reveal his sufferings (or joy) from the knowledge that C, D and E enjoy so much more. Individual A's welfare in y might be achieved at the cost of polluting the atmosphere of C, D and E. Do the numbers reflect the externality? Supposing that all four social states are connected consecutively through time, have the totals been adjusted for the possibility that enjoyment in earlier states diminishes or mortgages opportunities for enjoyment later?

If the answers to these questions fall short of a clear yes, welfare additions must be suspect. Even stronger doubts arise when the changes in the distribution of welfare between members of the group are considered. The most obvious comparison is between social states w and x where the change from complete equality to marked inequality leaves the aggregate unaffected. Individual E's losses (gains) are exactly balanced by the sum of the gains (losses) of the other four. Less obvious are the comparisons between w, y and z where changes in the degree of inequality are associated with successively larger totals of welfare, and with a smaller 'population' in the case of y. As between w and z, everyone is better off except B, and even he is no worse off. The gap between the worst-off and the best-off, however, is stretched. In the following numbers one simple measure of inequality—the *range* of each distribution—has been selected to distinguish between the same social states.

Comparing inequalities

	Social state		
	w	y	z
Total	4500	4650	5100
Average	900	1163	1020
Highest-lowest:	1500	1950	1950
Highest-lowest/average:	1.67	1.68	1.91

The first step is to calculate the average, then the distance between the highest and the lowest, and finally the ratio between this distance and the average. Although the average follows the total for most of the way, it does reverse the ordering of y and z. Averages are sensitive to population size, totals are not. In terms of both the distance and ratio, w has the least inequality. (If there is no inequality there will be no distance, and if the inequality is small the distance will be less than the average, so the larger the ratio the greater the inequality.) As between y and z, the explanation for the latter's apparent greater inequality lies in population size. Yet the distribution of z is very different—in particular at the top and bottom—between the lowest and the next lowest number, and between the highest and the next highest. This measure of inequality does not give enough emphasis to the extremes of a distribution. It can be replaced by one of the other more sophisticated devices which are available in the extensive literature on inequality. On such a sensitive issue, however, few of them escape criticism.

By contrast it may be objected that the detailed analysis of inequality is less significant to social welfare than the absolute welfare level of the worst-off individual. In social states w, y and z this happens to be A, although he shares the disadvantage with B in z. Nevertheless individual A is better off in both y and z than he is in w. (The possibility that he is better off in y only because of B's removal may suggest y offers the worst of all worlds from the point of view of this criterion.) Perhaps making him better off should override all other judgements about social welfare. Other exceptions to interest in the size and distribution of social welfare can be introduced. Suppose individual welfare was enjoyed at the expense of other individuals' liberties and freedoms, or was dependent upon the pursuit of what other individuals regarded as immoral ends. Then the usual, narrowly economic definition of the circumstances surrounding individual welfare would not be sufficient to support final conclusions about social welfare. In any case there is no reason to presume that the starting point for aggregation will be always a set of numbers. Individual welfare, and individual views about social welfare, may be represented by a set of ordinal preferences. Chapter 3 will describe the rules which these preferences or orderings are normally expected to obey. Unless social welfare judgements are to become the outcome of chance or accident, combining individual orderings to form a social ordering will also have to be governed by agreed procedures. Chapter 9 has more detail on aggregation and inequality, and Chapter 11 deals with the impact of non-welfare information, like moral disapproval and individual liberties, upon social preferences.

SOCIAL WELFARE AND NATIONAL INCOME

Reference has already been made under the heading of individual welfare to the prospect of aggregating changes in consumer surplus across all buyers of the product of a single industry to measure its contribution to changes in total utility. Such calculations are bound to include consumers with very different tastes and income levels, and are only comparable provided the falls (rises) in product prices always affect them in the same proportion. Otherwise, an event like a fall in the price of cheese, which particularly affects poor vegetarians, may not reflect equal utility gains to one like a fall in the price of meat, which merely benefits rich non-vegetarians, even though the total £s worth of their consumer surplus gains are indentical. Once more, these uncertainties about measurement by consumer surplus are compounded if the products happen to be strong substitutes or complements in consumption. Thus the aggregation of consumer surplus, or of changes in consumer surplus, is of no more help in finding a monetary approximation to the level of, or changes in, the level of total *social* utility than it was in finding a monetary approximation to the level of, or changes in the level of an *individual's* utility. Given that the concept was designed to deal with one industry at a time, everything else remaining constant, this should not be a surprising conclusion. The consequence is that economists are driven back to use money income as the approximation; only now it is the sum of all individual money incomes. National income is the monetary measure of all the goods and services becoming available to a nation during a given time period, usually a year. When all double-counting has been eliminated, and allowance been made for capital equipment used up in the process of production, what remains can be devoted to either consumption or new investment.

The connection between £s of national income and social utility is almost as remote as the connection between £s of individual income and individual welfare, for two sets of reasons. The first set mainly concerns tha absolute level of welfare and is composed of sins of omission and commission. Because national income relies on the measuring rod of money, and on valuation by market prices, it leaves out of account the contribution of all voluntary and unpaid labour, including that of housewives, and all those improvements to the quality of life which come as by-products from industry` including subsidised concerts and commissioned works of art. For that reason it also gives full weight to the products of those industries which impose costs on the rest of the community without paying any compensation, like pollution of the atmosphere and the decay of the landscape, when it should make a deduction. To an extent allowance can be made for these 'good' and 'bad' externalities, and £ national income adjusted upwards or downwards, depending on the best estimate of their net effect.

The second set of reasons mainly concern the more difficult and controversial problem of whether £ national income can be used to measure changes in the level of social welfare. A brief return to the case of individual welfare is helpful in trying to understand why the problem is so difficult. Welfare, or total utility, as a function of all the commodities the individual consumes (services taken for granted and savings ignored), will increase when the individual has more of some, and *no less* of any other commodities. This statement is unexceptional provided the individual's tastes do not change: he would gain no utility from more wine if he had just been converted to the virtues of abstention from alcohol. But it does not take the argument very far. Change is more likely to come with more of some and less of other commodities. In these circumstances, an individual is only better off if the gains in utility from those commodities of which he consumes more exceed the losses in utility from those of which he consumes less. The extra wine must compensate for the lost cheese and leave some utility over as a bonus, or else the individual is no better off, and might even be worse off. Whilst this statement is also unexceptional, and easier to interpret if tastes are constant, it makes little operational sense. In the market economy, the individual is free to spend his money income on commodities of his choice, subject to their prices over which he has no influence. He naturally buys those commodities which he prefers, or which yield him most utility. All that the external observer can do is to collect information about prices and quantities of commodities, and draw inferences about the connection between money income and real income or welfare. Supposing the observer to know all quantities consumed and all prices before (social state x) and after (social state y) the change, it should be possible to calculate whether the individual in y could afford to buy the quantities of the commodities he bought in x at the y prices, and still have something left over. In other words, he could still afford in y to drink all the bottles of wine and eat all the cheese he enjoyed in x if he so chose, and have some money income spare to buy more wine and/or cheese. An increase in money income which passed this test would indicate an improvement in the individual's welfare, provided his tastes were constant over x and y. It is not enough to look simply at the money value of his total spending in x and y (quantities multiplied by prices) because the difference might be explained entirely by inflation; and it is not enough to look simply at quantities because there might be fewer of some commodities in each social state compared to the other.

Unambiguous inferences about welfare are harder to draw when the same kind of tests are applied to national income data. Adjustments to the money value of national income for movement in the general price level seem straightforward enough, although it should be remembered that inflation and deflation often mask important movements in relative prices. Adjustments for population growth involve the regular use of national income per head, despite the alternative objective of keeping more people alive even at a lower standard of living. Yet showing that the money value of UK national income per head was higher in 1984 than the quantities per head of the 1983 national income, valued at 1984 prices, is not sufficient to prove that UK economic welfare was higher in 1984 than in 1983. Constant tastes and the commodity composition of income involve new complications when transferred from the individual to the social level; in particular, they become associated with the problem of income distribution. Despite the fact that the individuals who make up the 1983 and 1984 communities might be identical in number and in tastes, changes in their economic circumstances can combine to produce a differently preferred bundle of commodities. The community of 1984 may not be very interested in the 1983 bundle—wine and cheese may still be wanted, but different proportions, and by different people—so being able to buy the 1983 bundle in 1984 is of limited significance to the comparison of 1983 and 1984 welfare levels.

The distant connection between national income and social welfare or utility can be demonstrated in a model consisting of just two individuals and two commodities. In Figure 2.1(a) the national income situations of the community are presented in commodity (wine and cheese) space. Position y stands for the 1984 national income. Its coordinates give the total amounts of wine and cheese consumed by the two individuals, and the diagonal drawn through it gives their relative prices. Position x stands for the 1983 relative prices. Both national incomes have different commodity bundles (x having more wine and less cheese) and different relative prices (wine is relatively cheap in x). Thus their respective money national incomes can be calculated by multiplying the 1984 quantities by 1984 prices, and the 1983 quantities by the 1983 prices. Perhaps the money value of y is greater than the quantities of x at the y prices. The money value of y is certainly greater than that of z, because y has more of both wine and cheese and the relative prices are the same. But what about the social utility of y and x? Let point y* in Figure 2.1(b) represent the relative utilities of the two individuals, Him and Her, drawn in ordinal utility: the

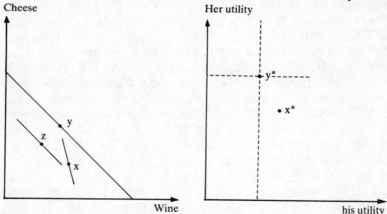

Figure 2.1: (a) Commodities and (b) social utility

commodity bundle of 1984 is associated with an *actual* distribution between Him and Her of the totals of wine and cheese and the coordinates of y* give their utility levels. Granting that the tastes or preferences of him and her are the same in 1983 as in 1984, x* should be in the north-west quadrant of y* to represent superior social utility. To be north-east of y* would mean that at least one of the individuals was better off, and the other was no worse off—arguably an improvement in social utility; and to be south-west of y* would mean that at least one of the individuals was worse off, while the other was no better off—inferior social utility. There is no reason, however, why the distribution between Him and Her should not have changed as the commodity bundle changed from 1983 to 1984. Different totals of wine and cheese in 1983 are associated with an *actual* distribution x* which is to the south-east of y*; she is worse off and he is better off. Social utility might be higher in y*; than in x*, or it might be lower. There is no certainty about the outcome, and no foolproof test.

The devising of tests which could disentangle the effects of changing commodity bundles, prices and distributions has long preoccupied economists. One especially popular proposal has been the payment of compensation—real or hypothetical—by the gainer to the loser from any change, to see if any 'bonus' in social utility remains. Instead of the *actual* distributions of x* and y*, comparison between 1983 and 1984 should be conducted in terms of alternative distributions as close as possible to each other, e.g. find a distribution of the 1983 bundle which is similar to the 1984 *actual* distribution and then discover whether it is to the north-east or south-west of y*. These are exercises to which Chapters 5 and 8 return. Meanwhile it is worth noting that constant tastes ought to include the choice between income and leisure as well as the choice between commodities. Real national income, in the full social utility sense, may have increased between z and y only in commodity-utility space. He and She might have had to work longer hours, and enjoy less leisure. The losses in leisure-utility ought to be set against the gains in commodity-utility.

REFERENCES AND READING

The argument about social welfare measurement begins in A. C. Pigou *The Economics of Welfare,* chs I-III; and continues in J. R. Hicks, 'The Valuation of Social Income', *Economica* (1940), 'The Measurement of Social Income', *Oxford Economic Papers* (1958) and 'Valuation of Social Income III—the Cost Approach', published with reprints of the other two articles in his *Wealth and Welfare,;* and P. A. Samuelson, 'Evaluation of Real National Income', *Oxford Economic Papers* (1950); and in *The Collected Scientific Papers of Paul Samuelson* vol. II,, ed. Joseph E. Stiglitz; and elsewhere.

Robin W. Boadway and Neil Bruce, *Welfare Economics* bring the advanced reader up-to-date with indirect utility functions and metric money measurements.

P. A. Samuelson, *Economics,* and Appendix, J. R. Hicks, *The Social Framework* and R. G. D. Allen, *An Introduction to National Accounts and Statistics* provide analysis of the calculation and meaning of national income statistics in ascending order of detail.

For the much wider subject of inequality it is probably advisable to try A. K. Sen, *On Economic Inequality,* and Douglas Rae, *Equalities* first.

On aggregation, and the relationship between the part and the whole, the economics student may be helped by Alexander Rosenberg, *Microeconomic Laws: a philosophic analysis.*

3 Preference Orderings and Choice

Individuals and households are always making choices: where to go on holiday, for example, which new car or washing powder to buy, what job to apply for, who to vote for in an election. Choices usually have important consequences for other people, even if they appear trivial (one washing powder being much the same as another) to those making them. Even a decision not to go on holiday, not to buy a car, not to apply for a job and not to vote in an election (where that is allowed) need to be recognised as significant choices. Provided individuals and households have the opportunity to select from a number of genuine alternatives, and the means to afford at least some of them, their choice is real and justifies some further explanation. It seems logical to assume that comparison and ranking precedes the final selection. Those who choose must be able to discover available alternatives and distinguish their characteristics. If individuals and households are 'maximising' in the sense of searching for the 'best deal', the 'best value for money' or the 'best available outcome', they will place the alternatives in some order of preference and choose the highest they can reach: they will buy the holiday package which combines the most attractive features at a price they can afford; they will vote for the candidate who offers a programme closest to their own beliefs, prejudices' and hopes. A holiday package, like a political programme, is usually a compromise between several objectives; in this case between location, climate, hotel facilities and price. The purchaser may have preferred a holiday offering a more attractive combination of features, but was bound to take a second or third-best alternative because of limited means. The voter may have preferred to vote for a candidate or party standing in another constituency or electoral district, but was forced either to abstain or to compromise on a next-best candidate or party to his own. All the attributes of

45

each alternative have to be weighed and compared. Of course decisions are sometimes made in a hurry, without proper consideration and upon incomplete or inaccurate information. Individuals and households may give up searching for the best and settle for the nearest and easiest alternative. In most of what follows, however, it will be assumed that choices are informed and not haphazard, accidental, capricious or perverse.

INDIVIDUAL PREFERENCES

A consumer might draw up a list of all available holidays together with their respective prices. A voter might identify all the candidates in an election by their party affiliation. Each represents one basis for the comparison of alternatives. Holidays are sorted by price, and candidates by party. Some holidays may have the same price, and some candidates may not belong to any party, so this particular relationship is not without its problems. Yet a start has been made on placing the alternatives in some order—holidays from the most expensive to the cheapest; candidates form the most radical to the arch-reactionary. Other ways of ranking holidays might be by hours of sunshine or by hotel facilities. Candidates might be ranked by their attitudes to certain key issues such as abortion or defence expenditure rather than by party affiliation, or even by their television image. The final selection of the 'best' holiday or the 'best' candidate, therefore, could be a product of several orderings based on different kinds or relationship. All these relations are expressed between alternatives in the form, holiday x 'costs more than' holiday y, or holiday x 'enjoys about the same amount of sunshine as' holiday y, or candidate w 'looks more honest than' candidate z. Technically the relation is a set of ordered pairs. The cost of x is compared with the cost of y, and the honesty of w with the honesty of z. Orderings of pairs, the binary relation, is the simplest and most commonly used comparison in the social sciences. Even a list of holidays with their average hours of sunshine is a set of ordered pairs: each holiday has a sunshine number. But there are circumstances when two or more objects need to be compared together. For example, a travel agent may wish to collect details of those customers who have two annual holidays. He will compile a list of ordered triples, or a ternary relation of the form x 'goes on holiday to' y and z: two holiday destinations against each name. Perhaps there are voters who can rank four candidates at once: w 'is more honest than' x, y and z. They will have generated a quadruple relation.

The fact that an individual can relate one alternative to several others may also be deduced from his ordered pairs. The outcome will depend on the nature of the relation. Take the relation, x *'yields the same welfare as'* y. What kind of binary relations between social states x, y, and z would it generate? Formally, a relation of this kind has three properties:

(i)   It is *reflexive* in the sense that x yields the same welfare as itself, just as the relationship 'has the same height as' implies that the object in question has the same height as itself. By contrast, the relationship 'x precedes y' in a procession does not imply that x precedes itself. Such a relationship is irreflexive. Some relationships are neither reflexive nor irreflexive. Although 'x respects y' it does not necessarily follow that x respects himself; he may or he may not. He may respect y and actually disrespect himself. 'Respect' is non-flexive.

(ii) It is *symmetric* in the sense that if x yields the same welfare as y, then y yields the same welfare as x. The relationship 'is married to' similarly implies that if x is married to y, then y must be married to x. Some relationships carry the opposite implication and are called asymmetric. For x to be 'younger than' implies that y must be 'older than' x. A relationship of the form 'enjoys at least as much sunshine as' is neither symmetric nor asymmetric. It might imply that x enjoys even more sunshine that y, and therefore y cannot enjoy at least as much sunshine as x. 'Enjoys at least as much sunshine as' is anti-symmetric. Finally a relationship of form 'supports' or 'likes' or 'hates' does not always mean that if x 'supports' y, y will 'support' x.

Sometimes it does, and sometimes it does not. It is called non-symmetric.

(iii) It is *transitive* in the sense that if x yields the same welfare as y, and yields the same welfare as z, then x must yield the same welfare as z. Transitivity also holds in relationships such as 'is descended from', but not in relationships such as 'is the father of'. If x is the father of y, and y the father of z, then x is the grandfather of z. This is an example of intransitivity. Relationships such as 'knows', together with 'likes' or 'hates' which caused problems for symmetry, are neither strictly transitive nor intransitive. Whilst x may know y, and y may know z, it does not follow that x must know z. Non-transitivity is used to describe these relationships. In many ways transitivity is the most crucial of the three implications, particularly for choices about welfare. It ensures that choices are logically consistent. If x is chosen over y, and y over z, then logically x should be chosen over z.

A relationship which satisfies all three conditions is called an *equivalent relation*; and 'yields the same welfare as' will therefore sort out alternative social states into equivalent welfare groups. It will not generate any order of preference: the individual will place conditions of society side by side; he will be indifferent between them.

If individuals are now asked to apply the relation 'yields more welfare than' to these conditions of society a *preference ordering* or a *strong ordering* will be generated. 'Yields more welfare than', in common with 'enjoys more sunshine than' or 'is more left-wing than', is irreflexive, asymmetric and transitive. An alternative cannot yield more welfare than itself or enjoy more sunshine than itself, or be more left-wing than itself; nor can x yielding more welfare than y imply that y yields more welfare than x. But if x yields more welfare than y, and y yields more welfare than z, then x can be said to yield more welfare than z. Any number of alternatives can be ranked by an extension of this exercise. What this kind of relation cannot deal with is equivalence of any kind. It must separate every alternative in the ranking.

Holiday locations with equal sunshine, or candidates of equal ugliness, or social states yielding the same indistinguishable levels of welfare, so that two or more alternatives have to be placed side by side, is not permitted. For these familiar situations a *weak ordering* is required, and the kind or relation which will generate such a ranking is of the form 'yields at least as much welfare as'. It is transitive, because if x yields at least as much welfare as y (either the same or more), and y yields at least as much as z, then x will yield at least as much as z (either the same or more). It is reflexive because x can yield at least as much welfare as itself. But it is neither symmetric nor asymmetric because the fact that x yields at least as much welfare as y leaves open the possibility that y may yield less welfare than x: it is anti-symmetric. In much the same way, if x is at least as clever as y then the only certain conclusion about their differences is that y cannot be cleverer than x. In the language of weak ordering, individuals can either prefer x to y, or be indifferent between x and y. Both strong and weak ordering are *ordinal:* they do not measure preferences in cardinal units.

If there are only two social states to be compared (alternatives x and y), and the relationship is a weak ordering of the form 'yields at least as much welfare as', the number of possible orderings is three:

$$xPy \quad yPx \quad xIy$$

By convention, x preferred to y is written as xPy, and x indifferent to y is written as xIy. Weak ordering thus includes strong ordering relations in addition to indifference. As the number of alternatives is increased, the number of possible relations increase dramatically. With only three—the smallest number of general application—they increase to 13:

xPyPz	yPzPx	zPxPy
xPzPy	yPxPz	zPyPx
xPyIz	yPzIx	zPxIy
xIyPz	yIzPx	
xIzPy		
xIyIz		

There are now six strong ordering relations and seven relations which involve weak ordering. When indifference is involved the alternatives can be written down in more than one way, e.g. zIyIx provides the same information as xIyIz, and xIyPz the same as yIxPz. In checking that 13 relations exhaust the possibilities, a pictorial representation may help:

```
x    x    y    y    z    z
y    z    z    x    x    y
z    y    x    z    y    x

        x    y    z
        yz   zx   xy

        xy   yz   xz
        z    x    y

              xyz
```

Placing an alternative immediately above another indicates preference, and placing them side by side indicates indifference. Those alternatives which can be arranged in columns of descending preference have irreflexive, asymmetric and transitive relations; and those which can only be arranged horizontally have reflexive, anti-symmetric and transitive relations. As the pictoral representation confirms xPyIz implies xPz, and xIyPz implies xPz. Two things are worthy of note for further reference: nothing has yet been said about the number of individuals who might be part of the choice procedure, and each individual has one actual ordering of the 13 at any point of time, although he may change his mind over time.

To complete this explanation of rational individual choice, two further assumptions are required. The first concerns the range of alternatives to be compared, or rather the range of comparison itself. If it is assumed that individuals can rank all the alternatives in some way, then the ordering is said to be *complete*. A partial ordering, on the other hand, may satisfy all the conditions for preference or indifference over some range of alternatives while leaving others out of the comparison altogether. The ordering relation will have gaps in which no conditions seem to be satisfied. Consumers, for example, would not be able to compare some holidays, and voters would not be able to compare some candidates, because they had inadequate information about them or because they were unsure of their judgements about them. As far as the other holidays or candidates were concerned, however, comparison could be made and relative preferences determined. The second assumption concerns the derivation of choice. It may seem obvious to expect the decision about which holiday actually to buy, or which candidate eventually to support at the polls will be based upon the individual's ordering, but that is a crucial element in the concept of rational choice. *Choice* must be determined by *ordering*, otherwise it will be random and unreasonable. Choosing a holiday or a candidate by the toss of a coin does seem a silly thing to do in these circumstances. Not choosing the best alternative, when given the opportunity to do so, defeats the point of the whole exercise.

So far no attempt has been made to see how individual or household decisions fit together, to analyse the social consequences of separate individual acts. Voting is obviously part of a social process, and each voter contributes, however remotely, to a public choice. Choices in the market also have important effects when they have been added up on the way the economy works at a national level. This does not rule out the possibility that individuals may take into account the interests of other people when they make their own, private decisions. They may vote for redistributive fiscal policies because they worry about the poor, and boycott Californian or South African grapes because they worry about exploited workers. Private decisions may be expected to have social consequences, although the private decision-makers may be unsure about how these social consequences emerge or that they will be the right ones. All such influences are permitted provided the private decision-making process follows the rules of rational choice.

SOCIAL PREFERENCES

Decisions on behalf of a community do not have to be made with reference to the preferences of its members. A dictator or oligarchy could order all the alternatives facing the community—having 1 of 6 preference patterns if there were three alternatives strongly ordered, and 1 of 13 if there were three alternatives weakly ordered—and choose the most preferred. The same choice could be made in an entirely random fashion, out of malice towards the general population, or from a feeling of responsibility or benevolence to them. But even benevolence, when it is of the form of knowing what is good for everyone else better than they know themselves, can run counter to the expressed wishes of its recipients. There is certainly no need to bother finding out what individuals and households want, to attempt the aggregation of individual preferences.

Whereas the normal expectation is for decisions on behalf of a community to have some relation to the preferences of its members, there is no general agreement about how the transformation should be accomplished. One problem concerns the number of possible preference relations. As the membership of a community is increased, these possibilities explode even more dramatically than they do for in the number of alternatives. Under the assumption of strong preference relations with three alternatives, the number of possible combinations jumps from 6 when there is one individual to 216 when there are three and up to 1296 when there are four. Under the assumption of weak preference ordering, with three alternatives, the number jumps from 13 when there is one individual to 2197 where there are three, and up to 28,561 when there are four. There only have to be four alternatives and four individuals under weak preference ordering for the number of possible combinations to exceed 6 million! Of course, at any one point of time, whenever a social choice has to be made, there will only be as many preference relations as there are individuals in the community. With three individuals there will only be three actual preference relations to amalgamate or reconcile, and they do not all have to be different. The problem is to devise a way of moving from individual preferences to a social preference that can cope with any three of the *possible* 2197.

Imagine a fruit machine with three display windows, one for each individual in the community. Each window can display any one of the 13 pictures representing the preference relations of weak ordering as set out in the previous section. So the machine can display one of the 2197 combinations across its three windows, e.g.:

x	y	z
y	z	x
z	x	y

Before there can be any pay-out, some way has to be found of transforming these three into one picture for society as a whole. Three identical pictures give an immediate reward, but the chances of their appearing are not very great.

The next problem, therefore, becomes one of deciding on the rules which are to govern the aggregation of individual preferences. Should every individual count? There may be arguments for excluding some people's preferences altogether from the aggregation 'machine', or for giving some people's preferences greater weight on the grounds of differential intelligence, understanding and responsibility. Should every possible pattern of individual preference be recognised? Even when transitive, there may be an attempt to reject so-called 'perverse' individual preference patterns as when a radical or left-wing voter gives first preference to a radical or left-wing candidate, second preference to a reactionary or right-wing candidate, and third preference to a centre or moderate candidate. Should individuals be expected to order across all attainable alternatives? Gaps in their lists of ranking may be explained by the lack of knowledge about some alternatives and of confidence in making judgements about them. A gradual whittling-away of the variety of information which is to be fed into the aggregation procedure will help reduce some of the difficulties referred to in the previous paragraph, but each step has to be tested against the standards of fairness, justice and citizenship of the community which the procedure is supposedly to serve. Restrictions of this kind can easily degenerate into the manipulation of social choices by an oligarchy.

The rules of aggregation will obviously have a bearing on the notion of democracy. Should agreement between individuals be confirmed only by unanimity? In practice, something less than unanimity, even a simply majority, is often allowed to settle social conflicts. Then trouble comes from vociferous and angry minorities. Should the intensity with which individuals prefer one alternative to another be allowed to count? If the majority does not feel very strongly about an issue, it may be sensible to allow the interests of a minority, who have much at stake, to determine the outcome. But intensities of preferences, it will be remembered, are very difficult to measure, and attempts to exaggerate their pain, multiply the exceptions and seriously undermine the majority principle. Similar dangers can arise from allowing desirable yet unattainable alternatives to influence the outcome between the remaining alternatives. A decision between two alternatives may have been made taking into account preferences for a third alternative. If that third alternative disappears, becomes unattainable, or if it suddenly ceases to have its previous attractions, then the choice between the other two should remain the same if preferences between them are unchanged. Only the order of preference should count.

The final problem of social preference concerns the rules that *it* should obey. Rational individual choice, based on a complete and transitive ordering of alternatives, has been explained. Does it make sense to expect and require social ordering to be so well behaved? Individuals can think and compare, but society is an amalgam without that capacity. Its ordering is artificial, created out of the often conflicting patterns of individual preferences. Inconsistency, whilst not necessarily a virtue, could be a natural outcome of such a process. Insistence upon a complete and transitive social ordering could impose an unnecessary and unattainable objective. It is probably true that a considerable amount of inconsistency and apparent irrationality is tolerated in social decision-making processes for a time. Major crises, however, do occur when these weaknesses are exposed and the search for processes which will generate more accurate and responsive outcomes is given new impetus. Too much disorder calls for containment. Why worry about rational individual choices if the social choice which encompasses them is quite irrational? All these problems will be explained in the next three chapters; first in the formal language of Arrow's impossibility theorem, and then in the practical examples of the market and voting.

REFERENCES AND READING

Although there is a lengthy and instructive treatment of preference relations in A. K. Sen, *Collective Choice and Social Welfare*, chs. 1 and 1*, the reader might benefit from examples and explanation at a more elementary level before embarking on ch. 1* e.g. John W. Bishir and Donald W. Drews, *Mathematics in the Behavioural and Social Sciences* ch. 3; Robert Mc Ginnis, *Mathematical Foundations of Social Analysis* ch. 3; and Wilfred Hodges, *Logic* chapter on Relations.

4 Impossibility and Social Choice

The difficulties posed by the paradox of voting have been known since the eighteenth century. An illustration can be constructed from the arguments of the previous chapter. Suppose there is a society comprised of three strong ordering individuals: A, B and C. They have to choose between three candidates for public office: a Labour, a Liberal and a Conservative. Giving an equal chance to all 216 of the conceivable combinations of individual voting intentions means that the outcome might be:

Individual A: Lab P Lib P Con
Individual B: Lib P Con P Lab
Individual C: Con P Lab P Lib

Now each candidate will obtain a simple majority of votes if put up against another: Labour, backed by A and C, beats the Liberal; the Liberal, backed by A and B, beats the Conservative; the Conservative, backed by B and C, beats the Labour. No clear, outright winner will emerge. Moreover, trying to derive a social ordering from the individual orderings runs into the problem of inconsistency. Applying the simple majority rule as a means of resolving conflicts between individual orderings gives:

Society: Lab P Lib
Lib P Con
Con P Lab

But that is intransitive. Labour should be preferred to Conservative when it is preferred to Liberal, and Liberal is, in turn, preferred to Conservative.

That there is something strange about this particular pattern or combination of individual preferences does not remove the difficulty. Each candidate appears once in every row and once in every column: the pattern forms a 'Latin square'. Each individual repeats a cycle of preferences by putting Liberal always after Labour, Conservative always after Liberal, and Labour always after Conservative. In consequence, individual C holds the oddest opinions. Apparently of right-wing persuasion—he gives his first choice to the Conservative candidate—he switches to the other extreme for second choice and only awards last place to the Liberal or middle-of-the-road candidate. No reasons have yet been adduced, however, for disallowing such odd opinions, and whilst their particular shape may be unlikely in the left-right spectrum of party politics, it could be quite natural in other areas of social choice.

Arrow's great contribution was to show that this difficulty was merely a special case of a general impossibility in passing from individual values to social choice, as long as the transition obeys certain minimal and reasonable rules. First published more than 30 years ago, his claim that this kind of impossibility could be formally proved has never ceased to startle social scientists. The word is familiar enough. Governments, it is often said, should never promise to cut taxes or make railways run at a profit because they would be attempting the impossible. But there is always an element of doubt. Perhaps a way could be found of avoiding the obstacles and achieving the objectives; the impossibility is not final, only a temporary limitation on human ability. By contrast, in mathematical logic there can be no escape. A proof of impossibility—that a square with exactly the same area as a circle cannot be found using only a compass and a straight edge, or that there is no such thing as the largest prime number—is a statement that it will *never* be possible to achieve the objective. Acceptance of the proof implies the end of the search for solutions. There is no point in trying to do something which is logically impossible. Arrow adopted the same method in his work, and although his negative conclusion is couched in highly abstract and theoretical language, no one has yet found an actual procedure which avoids one or more of his pitfalls. It is not for want of trying. After critical examination of both his rules and proof, and prolonged experiment with substitutes, the central difficulty in the concept of social choice remains. Impossibility proofs multiply, and social choice seems destined to be inconsistent or unrepresentative, even in the most liberal and democratic of communities.

This chapter attempts to explore Arrow's conclusion and his proof, using simple illustrations and avoiding most of the mathematical language. Hopefully the reader will discover that the impossibility involved is not quite so startling. The difficulty is pervasive enough—indeed, it extends well beyond the realm of social choice—but at the same time is rather familiar, almost an everyday experience, perhaps just another instance of human imperfectability.

There are several ways of making social decisions which are both simple and expedient. All the individual orderings could be placed in a hat and the winner drawn out, as in a lottery. One individual could be chosen as the cleverest, most attractive, richest or most selfless of the group, and his preferences would then become the preferences of the group. A small committee could be appointed and asked to make the decision between the alternatives on behalf of everyone else. For some purposes each of these methods is acceptable, and everyone can think of examples which work, from beauty contests to trial by jury, but for the purpose of making important decisions on behalf of society that affect all members of society, they are thought to be unfair. The unfairness relates to the fact that they do not take any account—or take insufficient account—of the views and wishes of the individuals who are affected. The outcome of these procedures is not reasonably related to individual preferences. So the problem shifts to a discussion of how 'being reasonably related to individual preferences' should be defined. What conditions should be imposed on the procedure of moving from individual to social orderings?

ARROW'S MINIMUM CONDITIONS

Because Arrow's theorem is so general, an understanding of its consequences may be strengthened by a contrast between his conditions for social choice and those which might be imposed upon an entirely different, neutral and partial aggregation procedure: student assessment. Suppose there is a need to determine the best student in a class, and the relative standing of all the others. Whereas Arrow wants to find a way of choosing between social states, this compara-tive exercise wants to find a way of choosing between students in a class. Arrow's raw data are the individual orderings of all members of society over those same social states. The raw data for the assessment of students are individual performances in a number of different tests. The full comparison looks something like this:

Social choice	*Student assessment*
Individuals	Examinations
Social states (x and y)	Students (x and y)
Preferences of individuals	Performances of students
x is preferred to y, etc.	x has higher placing than y, etc.
x is indifferent to y, etc.	x and y are equal, etc.
Aggregation device	Assessment scheme

Arrow argues that his conditions are the *minimum* anyone accepting the underlying beliefs of a liberal democracy would want to impose on an aggregation device for social choice. There may be other conditions which some people would like to add, but any aggregation device that does not meet his could be described as unreasonable or unfair. A reasonable and fair assessment scheme for students should not be arbitrary or unresponsive to their performance in the individual examinations. It should also obey similar, mini-mum conditions. Let these conditions be remembered as CUPID.

The first two conditions are called *collective rationality* (C) and *unrestricted domain* (U). On a strict interpretation of the requirements, collective rationality is subsumed under unrestricted domain, but their separation ensures the survival of the mnemonic and emphasises their combined power. Given the individual orderings of the members of society, the social choice from the available alternatives must be determined by an ordering. In other words, Arrow is imposing on the social ordering the same requirements of rationality imposed on individual orderings in Chapter 3. The social ordering must be complete and transitive although it can be strong or weak. Society must either prefer social state x to y, or prefer y to x, or be indifferent between them. If social state x is preferred (indifferent) to y, and y to z, then x must be preferred (indifferent) to z. That is the collective rationality part. Unrestricted domain means that society's choice must be obtainable from any pattern or combination of individual orderings. No patterns or combinations can be excluded, on the grounds that they are unusual, untypical, or belong to people who ought not to count. For example, in terms of student assessment, the final order of merit must depend on their performance in all the different tests or examinations. No restrictions can be imposed on their relative placings in any particular examination, and only examination performances matter. The tradition that always puts the professor's daughter, or the hockey captain top of the class, has to be overturned. Collective rationality's domain or rule is fully established.

The third condition is the *Pareto* principle (P). If every individual prefers x to y, then society must prefer x to y. Society must not prefer x to y if every individual prefers y to x. The responsiveness of the social ordering to individual orderings is easy to arrange in the case of unanimity. If one student comes first in every examination then it seems obvious that he should come first overall, and if he is beaten by someone else in every examination, he should not come first overall. Where there is disagreement the Pareto principle offers no guidance. It can neither be used to justify nor to undermine any procedure for reconciling conflicts. Just one extension is admissible. If the individual members of society change their minds (in the light of experience?) about their orderings of the same alternative social states, and if one alternative alone rises in all their orderings, then that alternative cannot fall in the social ordering. If students are given time to study and take the examinations again, and if the performance of one student alone improves in all the same examinations, then he cannot fall in the new ranking of overall performances.

The fourth condition is the *independence of irrelevant alternatives* (I). The choice society makes from all feasible alternatives must depend only on the individual orderings of those social states; and only variations in preferences over the relevant alternatives are allowed to have any influence. If one social state becomes irrelevant or infeasible, then the final outcome must be unchanged as long as individual orderings over the remaining feasible alternatives do not change. For example, if one of the students in the class is found guilty of cheating and expelled, then the overall ranking of the remaining students should be as before because their relative performances in the examinations are the same. But variations in preferences over irrelevant alternatives can occur. To take an example from politics, voters may change their minds about candidates who are not standing in their constituencies or electoral districts. Suppose the candidates who are available to be x and y, and the candidate not available to be z. Outcomes (either x or y elected) which obey this condition must not be affected by the entirely reasonable event of the voters first ordering x Pz Py and then changng to z Px Py. In both cases the ordering of x and y is the same, and that is what should count. The relative positions of x and z, and z and y should be irrelevant.

The independence of irrelevant alternatives also ensures that only orderings are important. Strength of preference, cardinal measurements of intensity, are excluded. No information about how *much* the voter prefers x to y compared to his preference for y over z, or about how *much more* one voter prefers x to y compared to another voter's preference for y over z, is admitted in the aggregation procedure.

A final consequence is that all comparisons become pairwise, i.e. are based on a binary relation. A complete social ordering is made up of a chain of comparisons between pairs of alternatives—x with y, y with z, and so on—but each comparison has to be independent of the other. Information about the ranking of one member of the pair with other alternatives must not affect the ranking of the pair in question. Society must *not* rank social state x above y regardless of individual rankings of x and y just because it is known that x is preferred by every member of society to every alternative *other* than y. Student x must *not* be ranked above y regardless of their relative examination performances just because student x beats every student *other than* y in every examination.

The fifth condition Arrow calls *non-dictatorship* (D). There is no individual whose preference orderings automatically become society's preferences, regardless of what all the other members of society want. If one individual orders the alternative social states, xPyPz, and the other members of society ordered them zPyPx, he would be a dictator if society ordered them xPyPz. It would mean that student performances in one examination automatically determine the rankings of all students in the final table of honours, no matter how they perform in the other examinations.

Arrow's conclusion is that there is no way of amalgamating individual orderings into a collective choice which satisfies all five conditions. It follows that there can be no scheme of student assessment simultaneously meeting the five conditions, and no Arrow-acceptable aggregation procedure for finding the best all round athlete in a multi-event competition, or for judging prize birds, dogs or pet rabbits when the 'ideal' bird, dog or pet rabbit has several different attributes. They all offend by contradiction. By trying to obey the rules of collective rationality, unrestricted domain, the Pareto principle, and the independence of irrelevant alternatives, they fall foul of the rule of non-dictatorship. In the paradox-of-voting illustration at the beginning of this chapter condition U was met because even the odd pattern of individual preferences was allowed. Condition P was met because there was no unanimity to be considered, and if there had been no unanimity, majority voting would have been respected. Condition I was met because if one of the condidates had dropped out, the ordering of the other two would have remained as before. Dropping the Conservative candidate would have left,

Individual A: Lab P Lib
Individual B: Lib P   Lab
Individual C: Lab P Lib,

and Labour still in the lead over Liberal. Identical results would have been obtained by dropping either the Liberal or the Labour candidate. The trouble starts in the intransitivity of the social ordering so that condition C is broken by the simple majority aggregation. Any solution to the impasse by imposing one of the candidates on the group (the first choice of one of the individuals) would offend condition D. In the trivial case of only two alternatives, the simple majority rule passes all the tests. As above, when there were only two candidates left, the outcome is rational and fully representative.

ARROW'S PROOF

The proof is general, mathematical and indirect. Instead of asserting an impossibility hypothesis and proving it to be correct, a possibility hypothesis is asserted and proved to be false. Whenever there are three or more alternatives, any procedure for social choice can be shown to break one or more of the minimum number of reasonable conditions which any believer in a liberal democratic society would wish to impose. What follows is an attempt to translate the proof into non-mathematical everyday language in imaginary examples: an industrial dispute and student assessment. Perhaps the loss in rigour will be balanced by a gain in understanding.

The proof shows that the satisfaction of collective rationality, unrestricted domain, Pareto principle, and independence of irrelevant alternatives implies the contradiction of non-dictatorship, and is in two stages. The first stage shows that if one individual is *decisive* for some pair of alternatives, then he becomes decisive over all pairs of alternatives, and so offends the condition on non-dictatorship. The second stage, by a generalisation of the voting paradox, shows that the satisfaction of the other four conditions must mean that an individual will be decisive over some pair of alternatives. Dictatorship is unavoidable.

Imagine a factory with a labour force of 100 men. A wage offer has been made and the workers can either accept the offer (alternative x), reject the offer and ban overtime (alternative y), or reject the offer and go on strike (alternative z). They have to make the decision as a group;

individual bargaining is ruled out. Each worker has a well-defined ordering over the three alternatives. One of the workers is the works convenor (president of the local), elected by the rest.

Stage 1: If the workers have agreed beforehand to grant the works convenor veto powers over their decision between y and z on the grounds that he has better knowledge of the employer and of the effects of their actions, then he has become *decisive* between y and z. To be precise, if the works convenor prefers y over z and all the other workers prefer z over y, being decisive means that the group must prefer y over z. On this occasion suppose the works convenor thinks the offer is disappointing and should be rejected, but that an overtime ban would be more effective than a strike, his ordering would be:

yPzPx (works convenor)

All the other workers are more militant and would prefer a strike to acceptance, and they think a strike would be more effective than an overtime ban. (For the purposes of the argument it is not necessary to fix their preferences between accepting the offer and an overtime ban.) Their complete ordering could be one of three:

either zPyPx
or zPxPy (the other 99 workers)
or zPyIx

Because the works convenor is decisive between y and z, the group must prefer an overtime ban to a strike:

yPz (group, by decisiveness)

Given that all the workers, including the works convenor, prefer a strike to accepting the offer:

zPx (group, by Pareto principle)

Now if transitivity is to be maintained by the group, rather than by individuals in the group, they must also prefer an overtime ban to acceptance:

yPx (group, by transitivity)

So the works convener has become decisive between y and x, in the sense that his preferences become the group's preferences regardless of everyone else's. The others either prefer y to x, or x to y, or are indifferent between them.

Care must be taken in manipulating the examples. For example, if the decisive individual had yPzPx, and everyone else had xPz and yPz (either xPyPz, yPxPz or xIyPz), making him decisive over y and z would be pointless: everyone has identical preferences over that pair of alternatives. Making him or her decisive over x and y would make the group have yPx, and by unanimity the group has yPz. But there is no way in which transitivity can help the decisive individual determine the group's preference between x and z: the transitive outcome for the group would be yPxPz. By contrast making him or her decisive over x and z would lead to a dictatorship result: by decisiveness the group has zPx and by unanimity yPz, with the only transitive solution being yPzPx.

Neither the existence of patterns of preference orderings that fail to produce dictatorship from decisiveness, nor the fact that workers in the real world are unlikely to grant one of their number such veto powers for very long, destroy the conclusions of Stage 1. Arrow only has to show that there are some preference patterns—and any pattern or combination must be admitted by condition U—which produce the dictatorship result. Equally, Arrow does not have to believe or require anyone else to believe that making someone decisive for any pair of alternatives is reasonable. The whole point of Stage 1 is to show that such a situation must be avoided because it can lead to dictatorship. If decisiveness can be avoided there is no impossibility.

What will strike the reader is the central role played by the transitivity condition. Whilst detailed consideration of this condition is postponed until Chapter 6, it seems unlikely that workers will worry too much about their group decisions being intransitive or inconsistent. Rightly or wrongly, in the real world, inconsistency may appear as a frequent and largely acceptable characteristic of collective behaviour.

How does the scheme for student assessment look in terms of Stage 1 proofs? Making one examination determine the ranking of a pair of students, so placing one student above the other in the final ranking because of their performance in this examination, although their positions are reversed in all the other examinations, would be equivalent to making it decisive. If there were three students (x, y and z) and five examinations (A, B, C, D and E), one example of their relative performances could be represented simply by writing the best student down above the next best, and so on:

Examinations:	A	B	C	D	E	Final ranking
	x	y	y	y	y	x
Student performances	y					y
		xz	xz	xz	xz	
	z					z

In examination A student x beats student y, who beats student z. In all the other four examinations student y beats both students x and z, but the relative performance of x and z is left undefined. If examination A is chosen to be decisive between students x and y, then the final ranking must place x above y. Student y defeats student z in all five examinations, so by unanimity or the Pareto principle y should be placed above z in the final ranking. Transitivity requires that the final ranking place x above z, even though z may have beaten x or they may have tied in four of the five examinations. Examination A is now decisive between x and z regardless of their performances in all the examinations. Unless there is some very persuasive reason for giving exceptional weight to examination A for students x and y—perhaps they intend to be teachers, and examination A tests their ability to make themselves heard at the back of the class—this seems a very unfair way to determine the final ranking of x and y, let alone the rankings of other students. Again the result turns on the insistence that aggregation procedures should be transitive. If student x *is* better that student y, and y *is* better than student z, then it would be very odd to place z above x in the final ranking. Transitivity is reasonable in this context provided one examination is not given special overriding importance for any pair of students.

Stage 2. Can the results of Stage 1 be avoided? If all

members of the group have identical orderings over all pairs of alternatives, there is no problem. The whole group can reach unanimous decisions. In fact the whole group is the largest number of individuals which can be made decisive for any pair of alternatives without generating the dictatorship result. But it is not the only number. Given the way dictatorship is defined, any number from two to the complete membership is consistent with the condition: and any number less than the total membership can be decisive in the sense of actually reversing or overriding some member's preference. Two is the smallest number that can be made so decisive and avoid clashing with the non-dictatorship condition.

Assume that the group of workers in the imaginary example make their decisions on a simple majority rule. Fifty-one workers will beat 49 in any pairwise vote between alternatives. Divide the workers into three sub-groups, each consisting of member(s) with identical preferences: the first has just one worker who wants to accept the offer but if it is rejected would prefer an overtime ban to a strike ($xPyPz$); the second has 50 workers who all want to strike but failing that think an overtime ban would be pointless and therefore prefer acceptance ($zPxPy$); and the third has the other 49 workers who all prefer an overtime ban to the other alternatives, but put acceptance as the worst outcome ($yPzPx$). The first two sub-groups make up a majority and the complete example can be depicted as follows:

Decisive number (51)   *Remainder*

1	50	49
($xPyPz$)	($zPxPy$)	($yPzPx$)

Because the majority all prefer x over y the whole group must prefer x over y. The 51 workers are decisive as between x and y by their own majority rule for group decision-making. The whole group cannot prefer z to y for then 50 workers—one less than the majority rule requires—would be decisive over this pair of alternatives. The group must either prefer y to z or be indifferent between them. As they have already agreed to prefer x to y, by transitivity they must prefer x to z. But an inspection of individual orderings reveals that only one worker actually prefers x to z, all the rest prefer z to x. One worker has become decisive over the pair x and z, the contradiction has been established. The group of 100 workers must accept the wage-offer rather than strike, even though 99 of them would prefer a strike to acceptance. Stage 1's result cannot be avoided.

Any number between 98 (in a group of 100) and 2 can be chosen to start the demonstration e.g.:

Decisive number (97)		*Remainder*
57	40	3
(xPyPz)	(zPxPy)	(yPzPx)

With this preference pattern the 57 become decisive for the group—considerably smaller than the 97 originally chosen, although still a majority. Arrow's non-dictatorship condition, however, does not insist on majority rule, and there is always a smaller sub-group than the number originally chosen which proves to be decisive, right down to 2. With 2,

Decisive Number (2)		*Remainder*
1	1	98
(xPyPz)	(zPxPy)	(yPzPx)

the trappings of democracy have been removed, and by decisiveness the group must prefer x to y. The group cannot prefer z to y for then one worker—one less than the smallest decisive number allows—would determine the outcome. So the group must either prefer y to z or be indifferent between them. By transitivity x must be preferred to z and the first worker has become the effective dictator.

It is important to remember in Stage 2, as in Stage 1, that Arrow only has to demonstrate his result for some distributions of orderings. Yet there is no requirement that they take any particular shape, or that individuals all be different.

Finally, consider the scheme for student assessment at this stage of the proof. Suppose there are now 10 examinations (A - J inclusive) upon which the ranking of three students (x, y, z) are to be based. Assume the following pattern of performances:

Examinations	A	B - F	G - J	Final ranking
Student performance:	x	z	y	x
	y	x	z	y
	z	y	x	z

No single examination is given special weight, but suppose examinations A to F inclusive are selected to be decisive for the ranking of students x and y. It is not that they represent majority of the ten, rather it is because they might cover that part of the course in which students x and y intend to specialise after graduation. Student x beats y in A to F inclusive and so x must be placed above y in the final ranking.

The ranking of y and z is a problem. Student z beats y in five examinations (B - F inclusive), and y beats z in the other five (A + G - J inclusive). Placing z above y in the final ranking would mean placing reliance on a smaller number of examinations than are being used to judge between x and y. Perhaps they decide to rank them equally. But then what about x and z? By the rule of transitivity they should place x above z. Unfortunately student z out performs x in all examinations except A. Examination A has been made decisive for a pairwise ranking of students by the rules of the assessment scheme, as a conclusion of the argument and not as an assumption. Given this pattern of performance, the examiners are pushed into a perverse conclusion by the particular role of examinations A to F for students x and y. Even with an assessment scheme entirely neutral between examinations, examiners would have some difficulty. Looking at student performance in this situation and using a rough majority rule, z clearly ranks above x in the overall classification (9 out of 10 examinations). On the same basis x ranks above y (6 out of 10 examinations), and by transitivity z must rank above y. Unfortunately with z and y they are back to the tie position (5 each), and no information upon which they can justify a firm decision one way or another. At least they may feel that the implied final ranking (z first, x second, and y third) would be fairer than the previous one, and the reader might agree with them. Yet in only half of the examinations have the three students performed in exactly this pattern.

Any aggregation procedure must meet certain minimum standards of reasonableness and fairness if its results are to be accepted by those who participate or whose opinions are to be counted. Arrow's five conditions seem unexceptional taken separately, but when combined together prove contradictory for many combinations of individual values which have to be somehow amalgamated. The logical proof implies that there are no social choice mechanisms in existence which obey his five rules simultaneously for all patterns or combinations, and no point in trying to invent them. Either the rules have to be relaxed, or a certain amount of inconsistency and unfairness accepted. The fact that democratic societies manage to live with what must be Arrow-impossible decision-making procedures suggests that their failings may be bearable. Relax any one of the five conditions, however, and the impossibility result disappears. Unrestricted domain, for example, can be amended to exclude all those combinations of individual values or orderings which cause the problem. The independence of irrelevant alternatives can be altered to admit interpersonal comparisons and cardinal measurement: student assessment schemes, after all, work quite well on this basis. Even the Pareto principle and non-dictatorship itself offer temptations to escape the consequenses of impossibility by pointing to situations in which democratic societies do sometimes act paternalistically. Unfortunately, avoiding general impossibility is not so easy. Arrow's five conditions were the *minimum* he regarded as necessary to define an acceptable social welfare function. Other authorities can and have suggested additional rules. Relaxing his conditions may be accompanied by the imposition of new constraints, and the development of new impossibility theorems.

The trouble starts as soon as it is recognised that amending a condition may also introduce undesirable consequences. Transitivity, for instance, may seem unnecessarily stringent for group decisions: but how much inconsistency can group decisions bear before looking ridiculous?

Paying attention to the strength of people's feelings and trying to measure the intensities of their preferences may seem reasonable, but what if their prejudices become socially destructive? Student assessment schemes based on marks or grades generally work well, but are they always fair? Arrow has proved and elaborated a difficulty inherent in social choice which extends into many areas of social aggregation.

REFERENCES AND READING

The major source is Kenneth J. Arrow, *Social Choice and Individual Values,* but it is better to approach this most difficult subject through Arrow, 'Values and Collective Decision-making', in P. Laslett and W. G. Runciman (eds), *Philosophy, Politics, and Society: Third Series,* reprinted in Arrow, *Social Choice and Justice,* and in Edmund S. Phelps (ed.), *Economic Justice,* omitting the proof section at a first reading. The translated proof in this chapter is taken from that section. Dennis C. Mueller, *Public Choice;* Allen Feldman, *Welfare Economics and Social Choice Theory*; and Sen, *Collective Choice and Social Welfare,* have useful chapters.

The idea and method of widening the scope of impossibility examples comes from Alfred F. Mackay, *Arrow's Theorem.* Beware the disease of notation: everyone has a different strain.

McGinnis, *Mathematical Foundations of Social Analysis,* ch. 1 contains digestible information about mathematical logic and proofs.

5 Voting

Voting is an old and familiar way of reaching decisions in a group when unanimity is absent. Many disputes are settled by a show of hands or a counting of heads, and everyone has some experience of this kind of social choice mechanism. Legislatures, clubs, trade unions and stockholders' meetings have all developed rules of procedure for the taking of votes, and their members have learnt how to manipulate them. Mass democracy is a recent addition. Voting can be practised by an oligarchy, by the members of the central committee of the ruling party, or by the college of cardinals, without being themselves elected by the 'population' at large. Even in democracies most executive decisions are made by small groups, by committees of elected representatives, or by cabinets appointed by elected officers. So it may be helpful to make a distinction between voting on issues and voting for representatives. Mass democracy—with the exception of referenda—has been primarily concerned with the election of representatives, and political parties have provided the link with issues through their competing programmes. It does not follow that all elections for representatives are based on universal adult suffrage, nor that issues are always decided by representative or unrepresentative minorities.

Experience has shown that the outcome of voting can be unrepresentative of participants or electors. Putting aside corruption and ballot-rigging, voting procedures which are honest and well conducted can still throw up results which appear to be unfair, arbitrary, inconsistent or perverse. Those who think they know who to work the system try to impose their wishes on an unsuspecting or complacent majority, whilst the innocent are shocked by the way in which their wishes appear to have been distorted. Some behave as if manipulation and interaction did not exist. The sophisticated voter, on the other hand, takes into account both the workings of the system and the behaviour of others.

With complete and certain knowledge about everyone else's preference patterns and voting intentions, the definition of the best course of action for the one remaining sophisticate is relatively simple. In reality knowledge will be incomplete and uncertain, and one sophisticated voter may be 'playing' against several others. A plan of action may be drawn up for as many eventualities as possible. The smaller the group and the longer the experience of previous voting—a small committee with relatively stable membership—the easier it will be to devise a scheme for manipulation, and the more likely that opponents will take appropriate counter-measures. The larger the group and the more recent its formation, the more difficult it will be to plan, and the more likely that the manipulators will be unopposed. For example chairmen who can control agenda and who have a casting vote, a cohesive minority who hold the balance between two equally balanced blocs, and those who have the time and stamina to stay until the end of long meetings, all stand a better chance of influencing events. Judgements about outcomes, however, imply that there are some basic rules for moving from individual voter intentions, and their underlying preferences, to the group decision. The usual justification for voting is that the social outcome follows *majority* opinion among the voters. The committee, legislature or meeting should not choose an alternative policy (or candidate) which was supported by only a minority of members of that committee, legislature or meeting. Another popular requirement is that majority voting be *neutral* and *anonymous*: neutral because it means that there is no built-in bias towards a candidate (policy); anonymous because all voters are treated alike. It follows that if a candidate or policy was preferred to all the other alternatives by every member of the group, then the group should elect that candidate or choose that policy. This is, of course, Arrow's Pareto conditions expressed in terms of voting procedures.

Majority voting appears as a defensible substitute for unanimity, in simple majority for most issues, two-thirds majority for 'constitutional' changes. The Condorcet criterion, for example, seeks to justify the selection of the

winning proposal, or the election of the winning candidate,
as the one which gains majority support in direct vote
against each and every alternative. Satisfaction of the
majority rule, along with anonymity and neutrality, however, does not guarantee the satisfaction of the Arrow
conditions. Voting procedures can break C, U and I; and in
trying to obey C, they even break P. A simple instance has
been given in the famous paradox of voting. But voting
covers a wide variety of electoral practices, and a fuller
examination shows how easy it is to produce different
outcomes from the same pattern of individual voting
intentions. These voting intentions, or preferences, will be
of three individuals, or three equal groups of like-minded
individuals, confronted with a choice between three policy
alternatives. Imagine the policy issue to be whether students
should be given subsidised lunches, and the motions for
committee or assembly decision are:

> x: students receive 100 per cent subsidised lunches
> y: students receive 50 per cent subsidised lunches
> z: students pay full cost prices for their lunches

Individual voters, or groups of voters, are then given the
cyclical preferences of:

> A: xPyPz
> B: yPzPx
> C: zPxPy

In what order should the motions be taken? How should the
voting proceed?

PAIRWISE MAJORITY VOTING

The natural place to begin is where each issue is put against
another, two at a time, until a winner emerges. Previous
analysis of preference orderings and binary relations points
to this procedure. Yet as any chairman knows who has
attempted to conduct a meeting when inconsistent motions
are being debated, and who has not come prepared with a
copy of an appropriate handbook, there are many ways to

produce chaos. One disciplined procedure is for someone to propose 'x be adopted' and for a vote to be taken on x against the rest (y and z). If x is carried, that is the end of the matter. If x is defeated then the matter is settled on a vote between y and z. With the particular voting intentions of the present electorate the outcome, with 'x be adopted' put first, will be.

x against yz gives not x
y against z gives y

Individuals or groups B and C will vote against the original motion, and A and B will vote for y rather than z. Half-subsidised lunches need not be the outcome. If the original motion were 'y be adopted' then:

y against xz gives not y
x against z gives z

Economic lunches can also be avoided. If the original were 'z be adopted' then:

z against xy gives not z
x against y gives x

Such inconsistency is open to manipulation. The chairman, were he a fanatical believer in free lunches, could try to put the motion 'z be adopted' before anyone realised what was going on.

A second disciplined procedure is to accept an amendment. If the amendment is defeated a vote can be taken on the original motion and another amendment. If the amendment is carried a vote can be taken between the amended motion and the other amendment.

When x is the original motion and 'substitute y' the first amendment, voters A and C combine to select x. In the run-off between x and z, voters B and C combine to select z as the final winner:

x against y gives x
x against z gives z

Starting with x and z means that y is the final winner, and starting with y and z means that x is the final winner:

x against z gives z   y against z gives y
y against z gives y   x against y gives x

Once more the outcome depends on the order in which the motions are taken. Pairwise honest voting breaks the conditions of collective rationality and is open to manipulation by a chairman or anyone who controls the agenda. Changing voter C, or voter group C, from zPxPy to zPyPx removes the oddity. Now the meeting has:

A: xPyPz
B: yPzPx
C: zPyPx

No matter which order of voting is taken, y will emerge as the eventual winner. It has majority support at crucial links in the chain over both free lunches and economic lunches. The chairman has no way of influencing the outcome, and there is no inconsistency or intransitivity.

Pairwise voting is common in committees and meetings making choices between policy alternatives. Debates can be held, and successive votes taken, step by step through the options. The wording of motions to be considered is obviously important. Indeed the power to determine the wording of motions, given knowledge of how those attending the meeting are likely to react, can be more important than the order in which they are put. But most people would not be prepared to settle the issue of whether to strike, ban overtime or accept a wage offer—any more than they would the issue of subsidising student lunches—by taking the alternative with the largest (minority) total of votes. Manipulation, particularly when several voters become involved, can lead to outcomes no one really wants.

FIRST PAST THE POST (OR PLURALITY VOTING)

Choosing between candidates rather than issues is another matter. The electorate want to hear the candidate speak and answer questions at meetings or on television, and make a joint assessment. They do not want to vote for them consecutively in pairs. In the UK and the USA powerful support is given to a crude and effective method for choosing representative members of the legislatures, in which each voter has as many votes as there are vacancies, and the candidate(s) with the largest total(s) of votes are declared elected. Ballot papers are marked with a cross or a tick. In a public meeting a show of hands can be taken. With the cyclical pattern of individual preferences as above, there would be a tie assuming each voter goes for his first preference. Ties are resolved easily enough by tossing a coin, drawing lots or giving someone the casting vote. The non-cyclical pattern produces exactly the same result. What conditions are broken?

Transitivity is preserved because there is no social ordering to worry about, just a single winner. Unrestricted domain is admitted because the method works with cyclical preferences. The Pareto principle is satisfied because if the electors are unanimous about a candidate being the best, he emerges as the winner. No single individual's choice automatically becomes society's choice—tossing a coin or drawing lots is arbitrary in its selection—so non-dictatorship remains in force. That leaves the independence of irrelevant alternatives. Let candidate y die before polling day. In the absence of any new nominations the individual orderings should be reduced to:

Cyclical	Non-cyclical
A: xPz	xPz
B: zPx	zPx
C: zPx	zPx

The winner is z. Nothing else changes. Irrelevant alternatives have no influence. The social choice is derived from individual orderings between the remaining (relevant) candidates. Had there been new nominations, they would have joined the relevant set. First past the post, or plurality voting as it is called, seems to pass all the Arrow tests.

If true, this would be an important discovery. Possibility, and not impossibility, would be proved. In fact, first past the post fails the I condition at a deeper level. As a special case of those social choice mechanisms which are interested in

finding a winner and not a social ordering, it avoids many of
the problems associated with pairwise comparisons, and
with counting second, third and fourth individual preferences. Even when it is used to select more than one winner
in an election, so that each voter has as many 'crosses' as
there are vacancies, they can be avoided. Unfortunately,
some elections are split into successive stages of elimination,
and run-offs have to be held to find the ultimate winner(s).
When the route to the ultimate winner is allowed to vary,
the same set of individual preferences can lead to different
outcomes. A demonstration of this weakness must await
Chapter 6, where the more general case is considered. In the
meantime there are two other major characteristics of first
past the post voting methods to consider: non-majority
outcomes and liability to manipulation.

Having the largest total of votes does not ensure that the
winner has more votes than his defeated opponents put
together. Representatives can be elected on minority votes.
Three is too small a number of electors to illustrate this
consequence convincingly so the example has to be expanded. Let the electorate be increased to 42 and the
candidates to four. Four groups of voters (A, B, C and D)
have common preferences between candidates x, y, z and w:

Voter group A: (12 voters)	xPyPwPz
Voter group B: (11 voters)	zPxPyPw
Voter group C: (10 voters)	yPwPzPx
Voter group D: (9 voters)	wPzPxPy

On a first past the post method of counting, candidate x will
be chosen with 12 votes, and candidates y, z and w will be
rejected with 11, 10 and 9 votes respectively. The winner does
not have majority support, indeed 30 voters out of an
electorate of 42 would prefer another candidate. In an
election to fill two vacant seats, the 42 voters would have a
total of 84 votes to award and candidates x and y would be
victorious. Assuming that each group of voters support their

first and second preferences, x will receive 23 votes, y 22, z 20 and w 19. Once more, the victors do not have majority support. On the other side of the account, it has to be granted that there is no inconsistency or collective irrationality about the result. It is just not very representative.

Unlikely as it seems, first past the post methods just might be applied to choices between alternative policies. A Sunday school might decide where to spend its annual outing—at the seaside, climbing a mountain, or visiting a museum—by taking a vote and choosing the option with the largest total of support. Its members might not even notice, or mind too much if they did, that a majority actually prefer to climb a mountain rather than visit the seaside, although the single largest group of members put a visit to the seaside as their favourite outing. Where policies are interrelated and possibly cumulative, such consequences are unlikely to be ignored. Committees and legislatures, even when their members are elected on a first past the post basis, adopt pairwise voting to produce their own decisions; and large meetings, like the annual conferences of trade unions or political parties, reduce the several proposals of the delegates to a limited number of substantive motions and amendments so as to facilitate similar balloting. It is partly a question of achieving effective debate and partly a question of avoiding a lengthy and potentially confusing series of votes. The outcomes might be inconsistent, but at least the participants think they know what they are deciding and why.

First past the post methods come into their own when elections of representatives are conducted by political parties, and when the electors have well-established party loyalties. The previous example of 42 electors makes better sense if there are four parties competing for the one vacant seat, and candidates x, y, z and w are each nominated by a different party. Voter group A could then be described as being loyal to the x candidate's party, and so on. Voter group A and their party achieve victory. But given two seats to fill, it makes no sense for the parties to nominate one candidate. Taking x and y to be candidates of one party, and z and w the candidates of the other, voter groups A and D behave well because they put them either as first or second preference. Voter groups B and C do not behave well. It is not clear which party they support, for their first preferences are given for a candidate of one party and their second preferences to a candidate of the other. Yet in spite of 'splits in the ticket' the result is a clean sweep by the x and y party: x has 23 votes, y 22, z 20 and w 19. A substantial number of voters (20) fail to get their leading candidates elected; and the majority of the electorate (voter groups B, C and D, 30 voters in all) would have preferred another candidate to *one* of those elected. Strong party loyalties, of course, should not allow electors to distinguish between candidates of their own party. Differences of character or temperament, stands on non-party issues, and attempts to produce a more politically-balanced committee or legislature are not supposed to influence voter preferences. It is easier to push this attitude in single-seat constituencies or electoral districts, thereby making the launching of third parties or independent candidates very difficult. Admittedly, the use of primaries allows the elimination of unpopular party nominees, but when the main election comes the voters are seldom asked about anything other than their party loyalty, i.e. no one is interested in their second, third or fourth preferences.

Second preferences are important in the manipulation of first past the post outcomes. Group D voters in the example might well give up hope of ever seeing their first preference (w) candidate in the winning position. With knowledge of how all the other groups will vote, they could engineer victory for their second preferences candidate (z) by joining forces with group B voters. In a single-seated election the result would be:

Simple voting	*Sophisticated voting*
x=12	x=12
z=11	z=20
y=10	y=10
w= 9	
————————	————————
x elected	z elected

Different outcomes have been derived from the same set of individual preferences, which is a violation of condition I.

But it would be difficult to argue that the result of sophisticated voting is less democratic or more unfair than the result of simple voting. Candidate z is not noticeably lower in the individual orderings than candidate x. The margin of victory is wider for z, although still an overall minority. Group D voters are not behaving dishonestly, only making intelligent use of a system which denies them their first preference. Unfortunately, other groups could try a similar tactic, and outcome of their combined efforts might be less attractive.

RANK ORDER METHODS

One way of taking into account the whole range of voters' opinions is to invite them to place all candidates on the ballot paper in order of preference. Following the Borda criterion, for example, a scoring scheme can be applied which awards marks according to the positions of the candidates on the voters' ballot papers, and the candidate(s) with the highest total mark(s) is (are) declared elected. With four candidates, first preferences would be awarded a mark of 3 (there being three candidates beneath them in positions of lower preference), second preferences a mark of 2, third preferences a mark of 1, and fourth preferences 0. Applying this scheme to the preference patterns of the 42 voters gives:

Candidate: Voter group:	x	y	w	z
A (12)	36	24	12	0
B (11)	22	11	0	33
C (10)	0	30	20	10
D (9)	9	0	27	18
	67	65	59	61

Scoring: 1st preference: 3 points
2nd preference: 2 points
3rd preference: 1 point
4th preference: 0 points

As before candidate x emerges as the winner if one seat is to be filled, and x and y if two seats are to be filled. More voters place x as first preference than any other single candidate, and the second largest group of voters place him as their second preference. Indeed, the only point of substituting point-scoring for first past the post method in this example is to confirm x's support in spite of the fact that he does not receive a majority of first preferences. Like first past the post methods, the outcome is consistent and transitive.

A similar argument can be used in the case of y's superiority over w and z. The margin of superiority, however, is equally narrow and the depth of support less convincing. Moreover it is still true that a large majority of the electorate would prefer z to x in a straight pairwise contest. The original cyclical preference pattern, where three alternatives are ranked by only three electors, will naturally give rise to a tie under point scoring:

Candidate:	x	y	z
Voter:			
A	2	1	0
B	0	2	1
C	1	0	2
	3	3	3

Scoring: 1st preference: 2 points
2nd preference: 1 point
3rd preference: 0 points

Once again the outcome is consistent and transitive, and no one can complain about minority victories. A casting vote, or a throw of the dice, is all that is needed to break the deadlock. (If the contest were between three alternative policies, the community might think it appropriate to accept such an equal division of opinion as a sign to do nothing, or search for something entirely different.)

It is important to note that point-scoring here has nothing to do with measuring the intensity of *individual* preferences. The ballot paper permits voters only to express an ordering of alternatives, and the scoring scheme decides only on the weights to be attached to first and lower preferences in the *collective* aggregation. Each voter's second preference, for example, will count equally in the addition of scores regardless of how strongly he feels about it. Changing the scoring scheme implies that society is placing a different emphasis on orderings, and for the same preference pattern a different result might emerge. Even in the 42-voter example, where each alternative takes its turn to be first, second, third or fourth preference, giving 2 points to both first and second preferences and 1 point to third preference will produce a tie between alternatives x and y (55 points each) and another between alternatives z and w (50 points each). However, there seems little point in worrying about such peculiarities. There are no good reasons why society should ignore the distinction between first and second preferences, anymore than it should score only first and second preferences and ignore the rest. It is more interesting and more relevant to consider point-scoring under changing circumstances of individual preferences.

An obvious change to start with is that of alternatives. Candidate x might die before nomination day, or policy x might suddenly become unattainable before the vote is taken. The choice now lies between the remaining (relevant) alternatives, not between them and (the irrelevant) x. Given the same preferences orderings as before, the pattern is reduced to:

Voter group A (12) yPwPz
           B (11) zPyPw
           C (10) yPwPz
           D (9) wPzPy

and the result then becomes:

Candidate:	y	w	z
Voter group:			
A (12)	24	12	0
B (11)	11	0	22
C (10)	20	10	0
D (9)	0	18	9
	55	40	31

Scoring: 1st preference: 2 points
                2nd preference: 1 point
                3rd preference: 0 points

Alternative y, which was the second highest scorer before x disappeared, not surprisingly comes out on top. The upset is the relative position of w and z, for now w pushes z into last place even though no one's preference between them has changed. Apparently point-scoring violates Arrow's I condition. Outcomes are sensitive to changes in rank ordering, and elimination can radically alter that rank ordering. The elimination of x ensures a *majority* of first preferences for y (22 votes out of 42).

Yet if the purpose of the exercise were to discover an outright winner in this sense, it might have made more sense to eliminate w. After all, w came bottom of the table in terms of overall points, with only 9 voters giving him as their first preference. With his elimination, z now emerges as the leader instead of x. The new calculation would show 44 points for x, 32 for y and 50 for z. Voter groups B and D now put z as their first preference. To find an outright (majority) winner requries another elimination, presumably this time of y. The final victor would be z because 30 voters out of 42 prefer z to x. Whether this outcome is fairer or more representative than any other remains open to question. It is certainly not the obvious outcome of point-voting.

Changes in individual orderings can also come about as the result of sophisticated behaviour. If the elimination of alternatives with the same individual preference patterns can produce different results, why not try to influence results by withholding or not revealing parts of individual preference patterns?

Suppose voter group C knows how everyone else orders the four alternatives and what the consequences will be under point-scoring. That x will be the winner under innocent voting is the worst possible outcome for them. Perhaps the biggest gap in their preference ordering is between x and the rest: they prefer y to w, and w to z, but not by very much. By contrast, they really hate x. In these private circumstances, and with the necessary knowledge, they might choose to manipulate their second preference, w, into a winning position. All it requires is for the 10 of them to mark their ballot paper with a first choice against w and leave the rest blank. The count then turns into:

Candidate:	x	y	w	z
Voter group:				
A (12)	36	24	12	0
B (11)	22	11	0	33
C (10)	0	0	30	0
D (9)	9	0	27	18
	67	35	69	51

By suppressing information about preferences between all the other alternatives, they avoid giving the others any points. It comes close to revealing the intensity of their preferences; being prepared to sacrifice their first preference if it means stopping x. Supporters of x are bound to find this result most unpalatable, and given advance warning of what might happen try to take counter-measures. One obvious ploy would be to persuade voter group B, who prefer z to all the other alternatives but place w at the bottom, to plump for their second preference, x. So the game could continue.

The eventual outcome of sophisticated voting could be either fairer or less representative than under point-scoring. It depends on particular circumstances. The notion of elimination, and the reallocation of the eliminated candidates' votes, at least suggest ways in which outcomes be made more representative. In particular, they suggest a procedure for dealing with situations in which no candidate or policy has a majority of first preferences. But so far the decision about which candidates to eliminate appears to be arbitrary.

PROPORTIONAL REPRESENTATION

The central purpose of proportional representation is to devise a method of ensuring that political parties win a share of seats in the legislature (or on the council or committee) which does not diverge markedly from their share of the total vote. Ideally, the shares should be in direct proportion to each other, so that the party with 10 per cent of the vote should win 10 per cent of the seats, the party with 50 per cent of the vote should win 50 per cent of the seats, and so on, until all the seats are allocated between the parties which obtain some significant number of votes. In practice discrepancies have to be accepted because of the continued existence of constituencies or electoral districts and the consequent division of the lists of party candidates. There can be no doubt that first past the post methods of electing legislators or committee members can produce extremely unequal shares of votes and seats (as has been demonstrated), and that the size and composition of constituencies can have a potent role to play in this misrepresentation.

In spite of its close association with elections contested by political parties, one version of proportional representation—the single transferable vote—is applicable to non-party or independent candidates and even to ballots on policy issues. Moreover the version follows quite naturally from the processes of elimination begun under point-scoring, only now there are *rules* for the elimination and reallocation of votes. Imperfect though its effects may be in terms of proportionality, the single transferable vote does facilitate the retention, for good or ill, of constituencies for elected representatives. Because this consequence is relevant to most versions of proportional representation, it needs to be explained before going on to the special features of elimination and transfer of votes.

The previous example can be taken as illustrating the election of representatives in a single constituency during a general election campaign. The 42 voters have to elect two (or 200) representatives; the four candidates belong to two parties, call them the 'x and ys' and the 'w and zs', and the electorate divides, according to their first preferences at least 22/42 to the former, and 20/42 to the latter (i.e. 12 As for x+ 10 Cs for y; and 11 Bs for w +9 Ds for z). Perfect proportionality is impossible to achieve, and the nearest and fairest division of the spoils would seem to be one seat for each party. Point-scoring, in most cases, yields a similar result. If the electorate is divided into two single-*seat* constituencies, the outcome could be very unrepresentative. Putting voter groups A and C together in one constituency and voter groups B and D in the other still achieves one seat for each party; but putting voter groups A with B, and C with D, means that the 'x and y' party will make a clean sweep. Perhaps it would be safer to conclude that the 'x and y' party takes both seats provided the parties and the voters behave according to their underlying loyalties. A constituency composed of voter groups B and C still might produce a majority for the 'w and z' party if x were (foolishly) nominated by the 'x and y' party and z (sensibly) nominated by the 'w and z' party. Nevertheless most of the time single-seat constituencies are liable to produce the most unrepresentative results and remain inappropriate for schemes of proportional representation. Only where no candidate has a simple majority of first preferences can the single transferable vote, along with point-scoring and preference-voting, have relevance in a single-seat constituency. (It is used in Australia for electing members of the House of Representatives.)

Under the single transferable vote method electors are asked to place all candidates in order of preference on the ballot paper. First preferences are sorted for each candidate and the totals examined to determine whether there are any outright winners. The test for an outright winner, and for any subsequently elected candidate, is the achievement of a 'quota' or 'minimum price' depending on the number of votes cast and the number of seats to be filled. Thus the electorate can be divided into any number of multi-seat constituencies, and a link retained between constituent and representative. The formula for the quota is:

$$\frac{\text{No of votes}}{\text{No.of seats}+1} +1$$

When there are 42 voters and two seats to be filled, the minimum price that has to be paid will be:

$$\frac{42}{2+1} +1=15$$

By implication, the winning candidates will have a clear majority of votes counted at the final stage (not necessarily of first preferences) between them, i.e. 30/42. If there is a winner at the outset, the *surplus* of his votes *above the quota* are distributed among (or transferred to) the other candidates in proportion to the second preferences recorded on every ballot paper which he heads. If there is no surplus, or no outright winner, the candidate with the lowest total of votes is eliminated and *all* his votes distributed among the other candidates according to the second preferences recorded. (Where second preferences are given to a candidate already elected or eliminated then third or even fourth preferences might be involved.) This system of counting continues until all seats are filled. In the unlikely event of a similar method being tried in a single-seat election, it will confirm that the winning candidate has majority support by eliminating the least successful and distributing his votes according to second preferences. (The quota in this case will be at least half the votes.) Similar arguments apply, in principle, to choices between alternative policies. Why shouldn't chosen policies—and there could be more than one in force at the same time—be seen to receive proportionately more support than rejected ones? (The method is really one of simple alternative voting.)

An attempt can now be made to test the single transferable vote method out on the familiar example. Each voter is asked to mark the four candidates (1, 2, 3, 4) on the ballot paper in descending order of preference. The result will be as follows:

Single transferable vote

	Voter group A (12 votes)	Voter group B (11 votes)	Voter group C (10 votes)	Voter group D (9 votes)
1	x	z	y	w
2	y	x	w	z
3	w	y	z	x
4	z	w	x	y

2 seats to be filled, 4 candidates, 42 voters
Quota=15

1st count: first preferences
           x = 12
           y = 10
           z = 11
           w = 0
           ──
           42

No candidate elected

2nd count: elimination of w and transfer of his votes (all of w's second preferences go to z)
           x = 12
           y = 10
           z = 20
           ──
           42

z elected

3rd count: transfer of z's 5 surplus votes (all of z's 5 surplus preferences and all of w's third preferences go to x)
           x = 17
           y = 10
           (z = 15)
           ──
           42

x elected

Result: x and z elected

Three points are worth mentioning about how this example works out: although z was the first candidate to be elected and y was defeated, 22 of the 42 members of the electorate still prefer y to z in a straight comparison; at every stage of the count there were just 42 votes because each elector is only allowed one vote; and the fact that all of z's 20 votes at the second stage of the count have second (or third) preferences going to x makes the calculation of how to allocate his surplus of 5 very simple.

As before, the changed circumstances of x dying before nomination day can be examined. With x eliminated the preference pattern contracts to:

	A (12)	B (11)	C (10)	D (9)
1	y	z	y	w
2	w	y	w	z
3	z	w	z	y

2 seats to be filled, 3 candidates, 42 voters.
Quota=15

1st count: first preferences

$$y=22$$
$$z=11$$
$$w=\underline{\ \ 9}$$
$$42$$

y elected

2nd count: transfer of y's surplus 7 votes
(all of y's 22 votes have w as second preference)
$$(y=15)$$
$$z=11$$
$$w=\underline{16}$$
$$42$$

w elected

Result: y and w elected

So the simple transferable voter method also offends against Arrow's independence of irrelevant alternatives condition. The removal of the (irrelevant) alternative x radically alters the choice between the remaining three (relevant) alternatives, even though the preference-order between them is unchanged.

Sophisticated voting can wreck equal havoc with the results. Voter group C can manipulate their second preference alternative (w) into a winning position by once again leaving their ballot papers blank except for a 1 against w. The example now works out as:

1st count: first preference

$$x=12$$
$$y=\ \ 0$$
$$z=11$$
$$w=\underline{19}$$
$$42$$

w elected

2nd count: transfer of w's 4 surplus votes

Because 10 of w's votes have no second preferences and the remainder put z as the second preference, the distribution of w's surplus looks doubtful. In fact, it does not matter whether all 4 are credited to z or only 2 of them (2/4 being approximately the same as 10/19). An addition of 4 will elect z forthwith, whereas an addition of 2 will cause x to be eliminated and z to be elected by default. (Group C's third preferences would have gone to z anyway.) The victory of *w and z* is a triumph for the minority. Nevertheless, their triumph depends upon detailed knowledge of everyone's voting intentions, of the procedures for elimination and strong group discipline; and that degree of sophistication may be scarce. It may also be watched by group A who could try to stop the ploy by offering to plump all their first preferences on candidate y. Voter group C would surely like to see their first-preference candidate win rather than have to manipulate a victory for their second preference. Whether agreement between voting groups is always honoured on polling day is more questionable. Predicting the effects of manipulation and vote-trading on the single transferable vote system becomes very difficult.

It is important to recall that a party-list system of proportional representation has no constituencies and counts only the voters' first preferences. w, x, y and z must therefore refer to politial parties, or more precisely to the candidate list of political parties. Although the names of the candidates on the national lists are published, the voters normally vote for parties and not candidates: they have no way of splitting the ticket by voting for some candidates on several different party lists. Making the 42 voters into 42 million (to give a little more reality to the example) who elect a legislature of 100 members, the result will be:

Pure proportional representation

Party	Millions of voters	% share of vote	No. of seats
x:	12	28.6	29
z:	11	26.2	26
y:	10	23.8	24
w:	9	21.4	21
	42	100.0	100

The allocation of seats is easy because there are exactly 100 seats to be filled by just four competing parties attracting roughly equal support. Each party now selects the first 29, 26, 24 and 21 names on their respective lists. Each could have nominated 100 candidates; with prior knowledge of their relative popularity 40 or 50 would have been ample. In a legislature of, for sake of argument, 438 members, and perhaps as many as 20 party lists, the determination of seat entitlements calls for complicated formulae.

One of the practical defects of the system is that it encourages small parties. Unless there is a threshold (a minimum poll share) sufficiently high to deter them, minorities find it easy to win representation. Thus there are no incentives for tactical voting or for pre-election agreements. All the sophistication and vote-trading has to be left to the *parties after* polling day. Faced with such a wide selection of alternative programmes, appealing to every kind of special interest, the electorate is unlikely to return a party with a majority of seats in the legislature.

In terms of the conditions imposed on social choice procedures, by contrast, party-list proportional representation stands up well. It responds accurately to the diversity of opinion and there can be no violation of the Pareto principle: unanimity would mean one party winning all the seats. Like first past the post, its reliance on first preferences means that there is no need to worry about the irrelevant alternative. Like first past the post, it is not necessarily a majority rule. An examination of the individual preference patterns (over parties) reveals an intransitive social ordering by simple majority pair-wise voting of xPyPwPzPx . . . Proportional representation, in this form, reveals instead a social ordering of parties in the legislature of xPzPyPw, which is transitive. By contrast, unlike first past the post, it is not confined to the business of choosing winners. There is a social ordering derived from individual orderings: individual voting intentions are translated into the party composition of legislature. So it *is* caught by its reliance on first preferences.

Consider the following individual preference pattern:

Voter group A: xPwPzPy
B: zPwPyPx
C: yPzPxPw
D: wPyPxPz

In spite of the differences in this pattern from the original, with everything changed except first preferences, the outcome in terms of party representation will be identical. The social ordering will remain as xPzPyPw (with 31 million voters putting party w first or second choice). This kind of consequence must offend the ordering aspect of the independence of irrelevant alternatives condition. If it were practicable for voters to rank the names on party lists, or to delete candidates they disliked, the outcome could be more responsive to their detailed preferences but sophistication, manipulation, and the irrelevance aspect would be reintroduced. (Israel uses a party-list system of elections. Many countries, like the Federal Republic of Germany, use a mixed system of party-list and multi-member constituencies).

REFERENCES AND READING

Philip D. Straffin jr, *Topics in the Theory of Voting* provides an excellent survey of many of the procedures in this chapter. Robin Farquharson's *Theory of Voting* is a classic of the pure theory, and Lord Citrine's *ABC of Chairmanship* is a classic of practice. Duncan Black, *The Theory of Committees and Election* provides much of the background.

Douglas W. Rae, *The Political Consequences of Electoral Laws* explores the detail of alternative voting systems, and William H. Riker, *Liberalism Against Populism* confronts social choice theory with democracy, supplying many examples and references. It is also helpful to read the 'Notes on the theory of social choice' at the end of the 2nd edn. of Arrow, *Social Choice and Individual Values*.

The modern analysis of manipulation in committees begins with Lloyd Shapley and Martin Shubik, 'A method of evaluating power in a committee system', *American Political Science Review* (September, 1964); and those not discouraged by yet another set of notations can seek enlightenment about social choice theory in politics by trying Charles Plott, 'Axiomatic social choice theory', *American Journal of Political Science* (August, 1976).

A most comprehensive source for parliamentary systems, including the methods of electing members, has been prepared by Valentine Herman and Francoise Mendel, *Parliaments of the World* for the Inter-Parliamentary Union.

6 Democracy, Choice and Intransitivity

Majority rule has been shown to run foul of collective rationality when applied to cyclical patterns of individual preferences. If only that weakness were bearable: there is much else to be said in favour of majority rule. Why should every imaginable combination of orderings be accommodated by the social decision-making procedure? Would it be such a serious relaxation of the unrestricted domain condition to outlaw unusual, rare or even perverse individual orderings? Alternatively, why not recognise that limited kinds of social intransitivity or inconsistency are regularly accepted? Why worry as long as society makes a decision, as long as a clear winner emerges, and individual citizens are participating in the process? What sense is there in expecting society—which is not of one mind—to behave as rationally as the perfect individual?

EXTENSIONS TO THE PARETO PRINCIPLE

Insistence on unanimity rules out all realistic change. Everyone must prefer x to y before society can be said to prefer x to y. The Pareto principle insists on unanimity when expressed in this stark form and treated as a *necessary* as well as a sufficient test of improved social welfare. If it were applied as a sufficient test (e.g. in Arrow's five conditions) and some members of society preferred y to x, then another principle, like majority rule, could still declare social welfare to be higher in x than in y. As a necessary condition it gives veto to (small) minorities who might oppose any change to the *status quo*. Those who stand to suffer (the few rich members of society) may not support a policy which makes others (the many poor members) better off at their expense.

The broadest extension of the Pareto principle can be achieved by the use of the form: if at least as many people prefer x to y as prefer y to x, then x is at least as good as y for society. Unanimity is included because if everyone agrees that x is at least as good as y—in fact, better—then society must find x at least as good as y—in fact, better. Unanimity tempered with non-opposition is included because if some people prefer x to y, and no one prefers y to x, then everyone find x at least as good as y, and so must society. Simple majority procedures are included because if more people prefer x to y than prefer y to x, then society must find x at least as good as y. The words 'at least as good as', it will be remembered, are a relation which gives rise to a weak ordering. Indifference as well as preference is involved. An additional symbol is required:

> if xPy means x is preferred to y
> and xIy means x is indifferent to y
> then xRy means x is at least as good as y.

Thus xRy implies either that x is preferred to y or that x is indifferent to y. It cannot mean that y is preferred to x. The extension is most applicable to the social outcome of pairwise voting. When equal numbers of voters prefer x to y as prefer y to x, or when x is preferred to y in as many separate votes as y is preferred to x, society can be described as being indifferent between x and y: x is at least as good as y. No harm would be done to the principle by either one of them.

SINGLE-PEAKED PREFERENCES

In the choice between political parties or the size of public expenditure programmes, exclusion of cyclical and odd patterns of individual orderings seems quite reasonable. Political parties are normally spread across a spectrum of policies from Left to Right, and public expenditure is normally available in budgets from small to large. Citizens— and this is the crucial assumption—are supposed to have preferences across these alternatives which are also 'normal' in the sense that a supporter of left-wing policies will prefer a left-wing party to the others, and a centre party to a right-wing party; and a believer in public expenditure will prefer large budgets then middling-sized budgets to small budgets, and so on. Opinion will not be polarised about the extremes left or right, small or large, and most citizens will put the centre, or the medium budget, as their second choice.

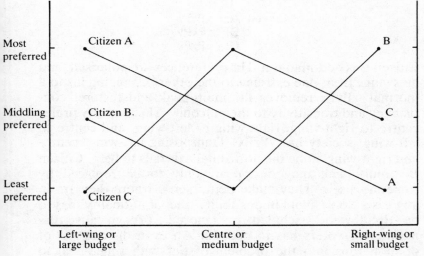

Figure 6.1: Single and multi-peaked preferences

This has become known as a distinction between *single-peaked* and *multi-peaked preferences* because of the way in which opinion, or preferences, can be pictured. Each citizen's preference ordering can be drawn as an ascending or descending line over an array of the alternatives as in Figure 6.1. Citizen A has pronounced left-wing views and puts the left-wing party (large budget) first, centre party (medium budget) second, and right-wing party (small budget) last. His line slopes downwards from the north-west of the figure to the south-east: an obvious single peak. Citizen B has equally firm right-wing views but puts the left-wing (large budget) second and the centre (medium budget) last. His line descends from west to south-east, and then rises again to the north-east: a double peak. Citizen C favours centre (medium budget) as his first preference, right-wing (small budget) second and left-wing (large budget) third. He is a centre-right kind of person and his line slopes downwards to the south-west and the south-east from a single peak due north. Converting left-wing, centre and right-wing into x, y and z, respectively, shows the familiar cyclical preference pattern:

$$\text{Citizen A: } xPyPz$$
$$\text{B: } zPxPy$$
$$\text{C: } yPzPx$$

Citizen B is odd-man-out. His preferences are polarised, and he swings from one extreme to the other. Changing his to a 'normal' zPyPx removes the multi-peak and restores consistency and transitivity to the outcome. The majority prefer centre to right-wing, right-wing to left-wing, and centre to left-wing: society has yPzPx. Transposing left-wing, centre and right-wing along the horizontal axis fails to help. Citizen B's multi-peak may disappear, only to be replaced by someone else's. They make better sense where they are in any case. So to avoid impossibility, the 'abnormality' has to be disallowed, excluded or ignored. (Technically, the number of voters has to be odd. An even distribution of opinion runs into the problem of ties with single-peaked preferences, and they have to be resolved somehow.)

Statistically the probability of multi-peaked preferences occuring increases with the number of voters and alternatives; more with the latter than with the former. Debate and discussion before votes are taken, and the preparation of motions on which votes are to be taken, tend to work in the opposite direction. Voters will be encouraged to divide on a single-peaked spectrum. Unfortunately, even single-peaked preferences can present difficulties to majority rule when more than one issue is to be settled at the same time. For example, if a vote has to be taken on the size of the budgets for public education and health jointly, there may not be a consistent outcome although each voter puts the medium-sized alternative as a second preference. Alternatives now consist of combinations of education and health spending, and those selected for comparison and decision do not have

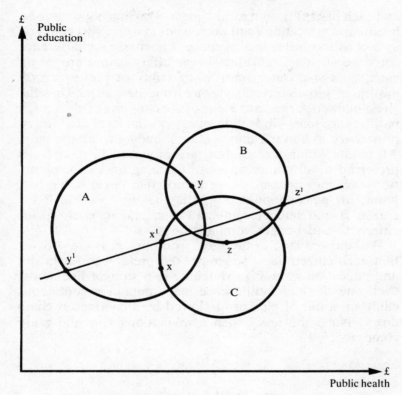

£ Public education

£ Public health

Figure 6.2: Majority voting in two dimensions

to combine them in fixed proportions, or in proportions which increase at a constant rate in the same direction.

Comparison can be made between budget combinations in Figure 6.2. Points x, y and z represent three alternative budget combinations. Alternative x has relatively low spending on both health and education. Alternative y has slightly more on health and much more on education; alternative z slightly more on education and much more on health. Citizens are unlikely to want spending on health and education to expand without limit. They have to pay for public expenditure out of taxes. They are also unlikely to want education and health to be combined in the same proportions. They will have different tastes or preferences, and each has a different ideal budget. Too much spending on health and education (and on education *or* health) could be as bad as too little. In this space, the citizen's indifference could be circular, reflecting lower utility or preference on each successive outer ring; lower utility or preference on movements in all directions away from the centre. Thus the circle marked A represents *one* of the contours of citizen A's indifference map—in fact, it represents the level of utility or preference to him of, among others, budget combination y. All points within that contour are preferred to y, and y is preferred to all points without, including budget combination z. Somewhere in the centre of that circle is his best point, his peak. Similar properties belong to circle B for citizen B and budget combination z, and to circle C for citizen C and budget combination x.

Without drawing in the other contours, it is easy to see that each citizen has a single-peaked preference for health and education spending. Marching in a straight line across each one of their indifference maps implies a continuous climb up a hill of pleasure followed by a continuous climb down. None the less, when combinations x, y and z are compared,

$$\text{Citizen A:} \quad xPyPz$$
$$\text{B:} \quad yPzPx$$
$$\text{C:} \quad zPxPy$$

These cyclical preferences will then produce an intransitive social outcome under majority rule. Yet all is not lost if the budget combinations are themselves on a straight line, i.e. if education and health spending move in the same direction. In Figure 6.2 three budget combinations have been marked as $y^1 \ x^1 \ z^1$ along a straight line. Point y^1 lies on the same indifference contour for citizen A as y; point x^1 on the same indifference contour for citizen C as x; and point z^1 on the same indifference contour for citizen B as z. Now there is no cyclical pattern of individual preferences:

$$\text{Citizen A:} \quad x^1Py^1Pz^1$$
$$\text{B:} \quad z^1Px^1Py^1$$
$$\text{C:} \quad x^1Pz^1Py^1$$

By majority vote budget combination x^1 is the final winner. (Society has $x^1Pz^1Py^1$.) Alterantives x, y and z are not on a straight line, and so cause impossibility.

Examination of these exercises shows that what prevents an outright winner emerging is lack of negative unanimity. In general, provided all voters agree that some alternative is not the worst, not the best or not middling, majority rule will produce a consistent answer. The person who insists on putting one of the political extremes as his middling choice, or who puts the medium-sized budget as his worst (or best) outcome, is supposed to be odd. Yet in some situations his behaviour would be quite normal. When a prize, a cake or an estate has to be divided between beneficiaries, private interest comes into direct conflict. Take the following way of dividing a prize worth £90:

	A	B	C
distribution x:	30	30	30
y:	40	40	10
z:	60	15	15

Alternative x represents an equal distribution between individuals A, B and C. Alternatives y and z represent unequal distributions: the first in which C is squeezed out by A and B, and the second in which A squeezes out both B and C. The individuals would order the three distributions on purely selfish grounds as:

A: zPyPx
B: yPxPz
C: xPzPy

Majority rule produces an inconsistent and intransitive result (y beats x, x beats z, z beats y) because there is no agreement about which distribution is *not* the best, worst or middling. A and B can do better than x (the equal distribution), B and C can do worse; A and C can do better than y (the least glaring inequalities), A and B can do worse; B and C can do better than z (the most glaring inequalities), A and C can do worse. Of course, no one is sure in advance which share they will be given. The identification of each share (which is A's, B's or C's) is a task separate from the determination of the size of each share. They might settle for equality in shares as the safest solution in the face of complete uncertainty, or they might act unselfishly and vote for equality as the fairest alternative. Neither kind of behaviour is in keeping with the assumptions of the preceding analysis, but either kind would neatly avoid the problem of impossibility in this context.

CHOICE WITHOUT FULL TRANSITIVITY

Collective rationality requires that there be a social ordering of the feasible alternatives, and that this ordering be complete and transitive. These apparent formalities have powerful practical effects, and their relaxation opens up another escape route from impossibility. Decision-making procedures can then be found which satisfy all the other conditions, including unrestricted domain. All they have to be is quasi-transitive and acyclical.

Quasi-transitive means that strong preference relations must continue to be transitive over three alternatives:

$$\text{if } xPy \text{ and } yPz \text{ then } xPz.$$

Weak ordering relations need not be so consistent. A group may prefer x to y, be indifferent between y and z, and yet not prefer x to z:

$$\text{if } xPy \text{ and } yIz$$
$$\text{then } xPz \text{ or } xIz$$
$$xRz$$

Where chains of comparison longer than triples are involved, *acyclicity* can replace transitivity. Suppose there are four runners (w, x, y and z) competing for the title of the fastest athlete over 100 metres. For some technical reasons they are unable to run against each other in the same race, and the competition has to be settled in races of two athletes at a time. If they all dead-heat in all races, there is no title to be awarded;

$$wIxIyIz$$

where I='ties with' or is 'as fast as'. For athlete w to win the title the races must result in:

wPx, xPy, yPz and *not* zPw

where P='beats' or is 'faster than'.

It is not enough for triples to be acyclical. Another set of results might be:

wPx, xPy, yPz, zPw, wIy, xIz.

Dividing them into triples (w x and y, or w x and z) means that there is still a winner in each group;

wPx, xPy and yIw, so y not Pw
(w is at least as fast as the others)

zPw, wPx and xIz, so x not Pz
(z is at least as fast as the others)

Athletes w and z are the 'local' title-holders. But taking the four athletes together no winner emerges. Contradictions always complete any way of using the information from all four separate races:

wPx, xPy, yPz, but zPw
zPw, wPx, xPy, but yPz
yPz, zPw, wPx, but xPy
xPy, yPz, zPw, but wPx.

Both relaxed conditions employ the relation of 'at least as good as', excluding 'worse than' while allowing either 'better than' or 'as good as'. Absence of quasi-transitivity and acyclicity must make a nonsense of social choice x even if society does not have a mind of its own. Second or third best alternatives could be adopted by accident, or an unpleasant *status quo* defended on the grounds that there is no stable support for a positive (and better) alternative. Choice procedures which obey these basic rules, and from which a best alternative is always chosen, seem to pass all the other tests.

Suppose a committee were appointed to choose the best economist of all time. The field has been narrowed down to Leon, David and Alfred. Consider first the adoption of a simple procedure. If all members of the committee preferred

Leon to David then the committee would find Leon better than David; if some members preferred Leon to David and none preferred David to Leon then the committee would find Leon at least as good as David; and if some preferred Leon to David and others preferred David to Leon then the committee would find itself indifferent between them. How would it work without manipulation? If the committee consisted of two members, or two homogeneous groups of members, and their individual orderings were:

Leon P David P Alfred
David P Alfred P Leon

then the collective outcome would be:

David P Alfred (by unanimity)
Leon I David (by disagreement)
Leon I Alfred (by disagreement)

which is not transitive because Leon is not preferred to Alfred, but which is quasi-transitive because Alfred is not preferred to Leon. David is the clear winner and his selection does not offend any of the other Arrow conditions.

The same orderings can now be expanded by a third committee member(s) to form the by now familiar pattern which has caused so much trouble:

Leon P David P Alfred
David P Alfred P Leon
Alfred P Leon P David

Total disagreement about the relative merits of the three candidates can only have one result:

Leon I David
David I Alfred
Leon I Alfred

They are all as good or as bad as each other from the committee's point of view. As for the indifference relations, they are fully transitive. If one of them is to be chosen as the best candidate, it doesn't matter which. There may be something unsatisfactory about the way in which the cycle of preferences is resolved, and yet it obeys all the rules.

Unfortunately, the procedure is easy prey to manipulation. We saw in Chapter 3 that, even excluding indifference relations, there are six ways of ordering three alternatives. So with two committee members (Kenneth and Milton) there will be 36 possible combinations of individual orderings:

Manipulation outcomes

Committee member Milton

	LDA	LAD	DLA	DAL	ALD	ADL
Committee member Kenneth						
LDA	L	L	not A	D	L	?
LAD	L	L				
DLA			D	D		
DAL			D	D		
ALD					A	A
ADL					A	A

LDA (etc.) is a shorthand way of writing Leon P David P Alfred, and so the 36 outcomes can be written in the intersection of the six rows (preference orderings of Kenneth) and the six columns (preference orderings of Milton). If the same procedure is adopted as before then 12 outcomes are immediately obvious: four 'victories' each for Leon, David and Alfred when the committee is unanimous about the most preferred candidate. Where there is agreement, there is no incentive for hiding or distorting preferences. Where there is disagreement the point and effect of manipulation is quickly revealed. Take the first row. Leon 'wins' in the first two intersections because of unanimity. In the third intersection, although David is preferred to Alfred and is indifferent to Leon, Leon is preferred to Alfred. All that can be said for certain, therefore, is that the outcome cannot be Alfred. David is the winner in the fourth intersection (because D is preferred to A, L is indifferent to both D and A) and Leon in the fifth intersection (because L is preferred to D, A is indifferent to both L and D). In the sixth intersection either Leon, David or Alfred could emerge because of the committee's indifference between them all.

Now the uncertainties have to be resolved. If Leon is

chosen in the third intersection by the adoption of some rule to settle the matter (e.g. because he is younger), Milton can alter the outcome to David by substituting his preference ordering DAL (as in the fourth column) for his true ordering DLA. Milton manipulates the procedure to achieve his *best* outcome by dishonestly expressing a preference for A over L which makes all the difference *to the position of D*. Given Kenneth's preference ordering LDA there is no way in which Alfred can be manipulated into a winning position in the fifth and sixth intersections, but if Leon were selected as the winner in the sixth intersection—which is the worst outcome for Milton—a substitution of the ordering DAL would at least achieve his *second-best* outcome for David. That is, the outcome as in the fourth intersection is better because of the *relative position of D and L* in Milton's ordering. In the end, the first row of the table would look like:

	LDA	LAD	DLA	DAL	ALD	ADL
LDA	L	L	D	D	L	D

Milton gets his own way within the limits set by Kenneth's LDA preference ordering. (The alternative arbitrary choices of David in the third column and of David or Alfred in the sixth column would have given Milton his way to start with.)

Manipulation is equally effective in other parts of the table. It also works with a larger number of participants. But in trying to devise a procedure which negates such behaviour, one of the other participants (or a group of other participants) seems to become a dictator. (Favouring Kenneth and allowing him to determine the outcome throughout the table would of course remove Milton's chances of manipulation.) In fact, there does not appear to be a procedure which avoids this dilemma. By allowing quasi-transitivity to extend the number of cases in which preference conflicts can be resolved manipulation is encouraged, and another impossibility discovered in the inevitable dictatorship or oligarchy of the counter policies.

A social ordering of all the feasible alternatives, however, is not a necessary part of decision-making. The best alternative can be chosen directly from all the alternatives, as in first past the post elections, and not by a pairwise chain of comparisons. The committee might be asked to choose between Leon, David and Alfred without specifying any relationship between the winner and those rejected; looking at the three together without first assessing the relative merits of Leon and David, David and Alfred, or Alfred and Leon. If the successful candidate subsequently withdraws, the committee can always hold another meeting. Their deliberations might produce as an example:

Leon is chosen from Leon, David and Alfred.

In case the number of candidates is too large for direct comparisons, there will be provision for subdivision into manageable groups. The winners in each group can then be placed in a final play off. As an example, there are three more candidates: Karl, Thomas and Vilfredo.

<table>
<tr><td>*Leon* is chosen from</td><td>*Karl* is chosen from</td></tr>
<tr><td>Leon, David, and Alfred</td><td>Karl, Thomas, and Vilfredo</td></tr>
<tr><td colspan="2" align="center">*Leon* is chosen from
Leon and Karl</td></tr>
</table>

Choice functions, as they are called, are insupportable unless they too obey certain elementary rules. Arrow's four conditions—or something very much like them—need to be redefined. The Pareto principle implies that if everyone in society prefers Leon to Karl, society must choose Leon when Leon and Karl are the available alternatives. Non-dictatorship implies that society must not choose Leon when Leon and Karl are available just because one individual prefers Leon to Karl and all the others prefer Karl to Leon. Unrestricted domain can remain in the same form because social choice is still supposed to depend upon all possible patterns of *individual* orderings; and that argument also covers the ordering aspect of independence of irrelevant alternatives. However, the irrelevance aspect and the condition of collective rationality require rather more attention.

To ensure that the winner is the best alternative—one of the key rules—its selection must be independent of the path

by which it emerges. In other words, Leon must be chosen
whatever the composition of the earlier play offs:

Leon is chosen from	*David* is chosen from
Leon, Thomas and Vilfredo	David, Alfred and Karl

Leon is chosen from
Leon and David

or any other arrangement of the choice process. Transitivity
or consistency in choice can be interpreted to mean two
things: if Leon is chosen when Leon, Thomas and Vilfredo
are available, he will also be chosen when only Leon and
Thomas are available—a seemingly obvious requirement
related to a reduction in the number of alternatives
available; and, if Leon and David are chosen as the two best
candidates (the *two* best economists of all time) when Leon,
David and Alfred are available, David will not be chosen as
one of the two best candidates when Leon, David, Alfred
and Karl are available, unless Leon is also so chosen—a less
obvious requirement related to an increase in the number of
alternatives available. In terms of the height of mountains
both requirements are met: if Everest is the highest
mountain in the world, it must be the highest mountain in
the Himalayas; and if Everest and K2 are the two highest
mountains in the Himalayas, K2 cannot be one of the
highest mountains in the world without Everest being so
included. There can be no doubt about the relative height of
all the mountains in the world, because height is measurable
in cardinal units. In other dimensions, and in preference
relations in particular, these requirements may not be met
because every choice is based on ordinal rankings. Whilst it
may be reasonable to assume that the committee will
continue to choose Leon as the number of candidates
contracts, their choice could well change when the number
expands. Leon and David are chosen as the best candidates
when only Alfred competes with them, but when Karl is
added they may think that David and Karl will sound better
together than Leon and David.

It is possible to design choice procedures which obey all
the other rules, which reach outcomes independently of the
path of choices, which cannot be manipulated, and which

pass *one or other* of the tests of consistency. It is not possible to design procedures which pass both tests simultaneously and obey all the other rules. In any case, these procedures can produce some strange (and unacceptable?) results.

The 'cycle' of individual preferences serves once more to illustrate the problem. Take three members of a committee or three separately unamimous blocks in a legislature. Their individual orderings over *four* candidates may be:

Leon preferred to David preferred to Alfred preferred to Karl

DAKL

AKLD

By pairwise comparison and simple majority voting, the outcome would be:

Leon P David
David P Alfred
Alfred P Karl
Karl P Leon

The chain is intransitive and the consequent indecisiveness can only be settled by some tie-breaking rule. Any one of the *four* candidates could then emerge, including Karl who is Pareto-inferior. No one (no block of voters) gives him their first preference, and everyone prefers Alfred to him. First past the post elections (which are in fact choice procedures) produce a tie only between *three* candidates: Leon, David and Alfred receive one vote each; Karl scores zero. But this superiority of the procedure disappears once subdivisions of the candidates are introduced. If David is made to fight Alfred first, and the winner of that contest fights Leon second, and the winner of that contest fights Karl in the final, Karl will again emerge.

> *David* is chosen from David and Alfred
> *Leon* is chosen from David and Leon
> *Karl* is chosen from Leon and Karl

Of course, other subdivisions will produce other choices, by the same largest plurality rule. In other words, there is a path which leads to any one of the four candidates, including the Pareto-inferior Karl.

In this chapter relaxations of the C, U and P conditions

have been applied to social decision and choice procedures of a familiar kind to see if an escape from the dictatorship conclusions of the Arrow impossibility theorem can be found. Although considerable progress has been made, all the escapes have disadvantages and difficulties of their own which are liable to develop into new impossibility theorems. In the next chapter a rather different social choice procedure is examined.

READING AND REFERENCES

None of the reading for this chapter is easy, and some is very difficult. The modern pioneer of the work on multi- and single-peaked preferences and committee decisions is Duncan Black, *The Theory of Committees and Elections*. Allan Feldman, *Welfare Economics and Social Choice Theory, op.cit.*, provides useful figures on their consequences and they are used here.

William H. Riker, *Liberalism Against Popularism*, has a section on path independence. Amartya Sen is the main source for most of the rest: *Collective Choice and Social Welfare and Measurement*, essays 5-8.

The structure of the manipulation exercise on world-famous economists is taken from A. Gibbard, 'Manipulation of voting schemes: a general result', *Econometrica* (1973).

Two other advanced articles are relevant: M. A. Satterthwaithe 'Strategy proofness and Arrow's condition', *Journal of Economic Theory (1975)*; and Charles H. Plott, 'Path independence, rationality and social choice', *Econometrica* (1973).

7 Markets

Markets are a device for making social decisions in the economic sphere. They determine *what* is to be produced, *how* it is to be produced, and by *whom* it is to be consumed, without recourse to physical force or central direction. Whilst their natural habitat is supposed to be in the private enterprise or capitalist economies, they also have important roles to play in planned or socialist economies. Like voting they provide another demonstration of impossibility in social choice. At the same time they exhibit characteristics which may be defended or attacked on other grounds. Economists, for example, extol the efficiency of markets but are less enthusiastic about their equity. Efficiency is apparently compatible with a great deal of inequality. Alternatively, advantage is seen in the fact that their outcomes do not depend on the identity of the participants: anyone can buy and sell, compete and accumulate. There are not supposed to be any political, religious or cultural restraints. Even the moral worth of the trader is ignored. So opportunity may be maximised and success not always deserved.

The purpose of this chapter is to show how markets generate social choices; and in so doing offend against the condition of collective rationality. This may be illustrated by what is known to economists as the non-uniqueness of competitive equilibria, and has much to do with changes in the distribution of income, and with intransitive social ordering. Individuals have preferences between, among other things, commodities they would like to consume. On markets they 'vote' for them by offering money income in exchange. Each individual has as many 'votes' as his total income or claims on resources permit. Changes in the distribution of income, with the same set of individual preferences, will alter the 'votes' or 'offers' of identical individuals. The poor do not buy the same things as they would if they were rich.

111

Markets

THE IDEAL MARKET SYSTEM

In modern industrial societies specialisation and the division of labour have proceeded so far that no one can satisfy all their material needs without the willing (or unwilling) help of others. The great advances in production efficiency have been achieved at the cost of a segregated community, and some way has to be found of providing the necessary degree of cooperation. Sometimes people accept their alloted tasks and rewards out of respect for established practice, as part of an inherited network of reciprocal responsibilities, and this is one organising principle for economic and social life. Planning by governments with the intelligence and authority to devise and enforce economic commands represents a conscious attempt by society—or by those purporting to act for society—to organise itself. The market, at the other extreme, assembles a solution to society's economic problems out of thousands of individual acts. People cooperate because it is in their interests to do so, not because they have been told to do so, because they have always done so, nor because they believe themselves to be taking part in a social process. They need not be conscious of any public responsibility. So how does the market harness these separate elements?

To answer the question properly, presumptions about individual behaviour and motivation have to be examined along with other essential features of the system.

Self-interest
Every individual is presumed to know what is best for him/her, and to be able to choose the appropriate course of action from all the alternatives; every individual knows and can choose better for him/herself than anyone else.

Private ownership
Commodities for consumption, and at least labour as a factor of production (slavery is not included) are owned outright by individuals. The initial endowment of factors, property ownership, is a datum for the economic system. Individuals are free to choose when and where to work, how

to spend their incomes, and what purposes to put the commodities they buy.

Voluntary trading
Within the law every individual pursues his best interest in trading without restraint on the terms or the identity of the transaction. Every encouragement is given to private initiative in exploiting opportunities for mutual advantages in both production and consumption activities.

Competition
There is a large enough number of independent producers and consumers to ensure that no one trader, nor even a group of traders, can dominate or manipulate markets for factors or commodities; and to provide the incentive for each producer continually to improve the quality and availability of his/her product.

Decentralisation
The signals and incentives employed to organise and coordinate production and consumption are those of a price system—a system of relative (money) prices that covers every pair of factors and goods. There is no central planning agency to collect detailed information about the workings of all production and consumption units, and to issue instructions.

Amorality and anonymity
The pricing system should not discriminate between individuals as to their race, creed, colour, etc.; nor should it weigh actions according to whether they are done out of benevolence or malevolence, intended for the benefit of community at large, or only for private profit.

Decisions about what and how things are to be produced, therefore, result from the competitive interaction of producer's offers to supply goods and consumers' offers to buy goods through the medium of a price system. Decisions about for whom these goods are produced are based upon demand and supply in the markets for factors of production, which in turn are determined by the initial allocation of property ownership, acquired or inherited abilities and opportunities for education.

Self-interest is an assumption about behaviour, or rather a specification of the behaviour which is best suited to the market system and about which legislation or other formal methods of social control can do little. Although benevolence and malevolence cannot be ruled out, it has to be admitted that the pursuit of self-interest is a recognisable motive for economic actions, and a habit that can be socially conditioned. Nevertheless, voluntary trading, competition and private ownership do need social control if they are to be maintained in sufficient degrees of purity. Legislation may be required to create a favourable environment, to protect individual rights, and to prohibit certain kinds of activity. For the market system to work properly, there may have to be a strong government or public protective agency. Similar regulations may be required to prevent prejudice, discrimination and violence from interfering with the anonymity of market processes. A liberal democracy may not be able to exercise sufficient control if some of the conditions for ideal behaviour are undermined.

A fable may aid understanding of the way in which the ideal price system is supposed to work. Suppose three men on an island have nothing to do but wander about and eat cake. The cake is delivered to them every day by helicopter, in a daily 'drop' of three cakes in some combination of chocolate and walnut flavours (i.e. two walnut, one chocolate; two chocolate, one walnut). If three cakes are sufficient for their daily needs, because each man can only eat one cake, or because the sum of their total appetites exactly equals three cakes, and if they are unable to detect any significant difference between the enjoyment or satisfaction derived from eating chocolate rather than walnut cake, there would be no problem of allocating the drop – no problem, that is, provided there is no man who enjoys denying cake to another out of wickedness rather than appetite.

There would be a potential for conflict between the three men on the island if three cakes were insufficient to meet their appetites, or if they had different tastes for chocolate compared with walnut cake. Even if they had identical tastes between walnut and chocolate (e.g. all preferring walnut) and the helicopter always brought two chocolate and one walnut cake, it would be difficult for them to satisfy their needs without a struggle. That struggle could be settled by force: very simply, they fight until the winner claims enough cake of his preferred flavour satisfies his needs, and leaves the rest to the other two. There may have to be a second fight between the two losers, or the two may learn that there is an advantage in ganging up on the third. Extreme conflict might lead to murder, for three cakes go further when divided between only two.

Violent struggle could be avoided by programming each man with a built-in aversion to violence, or by dropping a set of rules along with the cakes with sufficient threats to enforce compliance: 'If you do not obey these rules you will be struck by lightning.' Allocation of cake might then be settled by races, or by games of skill and chance. The rules might specify that Tom was to have chocolate cake on Mondays and Dick on Tuesdays; or that the drop was to be equally divided between Tom, Dick and Harry every day regardless of its flavour. Equal shares need not mean that they are equally satisfied, for unequal appetites and dissimilar tastes are allowed. None of them needs be happy with the final result whatever non-violent method is used, but at least they would stay alive: unhappy, that is, provided they do not enjoy giving cake to each other, having been programmed to love one another as well as to be non-violent towards each other.

Instead of indiscriminate cake-dropping, however, there could be a system of individual parcels. In Tom's parcel there might be a chocolate cake, or half a chocolate cake and half a walnut cake, and so on for Dick and Harry. The cake total could remain fixed, but the daily drop brings a mixed bag of individual presents. With unequal appetites and dissimilar tastes, there might be a violent struggle to hold onto the original parcels. Again a more peaceful solution is suggested by the introduction of rules, this time controlling behaviour rather than details of daily consumption. Each man has to respect, or at least must not interfere with, the others' parcels, and accept his own. They are then free to swap cakes or slices of cake among themselves until they feel that no further swapping can improve the situation. Tom, with only chocolate cake in his original parcel, may offer Dick, with only walnut cake, a slice of chocolate cake for a slice of walnut cake; and the process could continue for some time, with slices, big or small, being offered in exchange, depending on the contents of their original parcels, their individual appetites and their preferences for different kinds of cake, until all three are convinced that the opportunities for achieving a better final division of cake have been exhausted. They would have reached a state of limited happiness by mutual agreement. Once the drop has been made, the amount and the terms of swapping are for them to arrange among themselves as long as they observe the rules. The rules do *not* specify the content of the final division.

Cake-swapping is an oversimplified and imaginary example of what economists mean by *pure exchange*—pure because it involves no production; the goods and services to be exchanged appear as from nowhere without effort on the part of the recipients, who are left only with the problem of reaching an *exchange equilibrium*. The 'cakes' of the example are the economist's commodities and services, the helicopter drop of individual parcels becomes the initial allocation, and the final division of cake becomes the exchange equilibrium or final distribution. Swapping is, of course, *trade,* and the limited state of happiness arrived at by the exhaustion of the opportunities for achieving a better final division of cake is reaching the *optimum* trade. Leaving the men to do their own trading, to seek the optimum on their own, without specific instructions about the final distribution, is to rely on a *market* solution rather than a planning or custom-determined solution.

If the goods and services to be exchanged have first to be produced the principle of the market remains the same, only the solution becomes more complicated. Now the men will find the ingredients for cake-making, (fuel, and the necessary ovens and cake tins) scattered about the island. They will have to find them, perhaps dig some of them up, assemble them and bake every day. They may find that cocoa is more plentiful than walnuts. Tom may have some special skills or aptitudes in cooking; Dick may be strong and able to dig quickly; whilst Harry may be just lazy. Perhaps they may be clever and interested enough to experiment, to discover new ingredients and bake fruit cakes as well as chocolate and walnut cakes.

To continue the fable, it would be logical to assume that the ingredients for cakes were not left lying about the island, but labelled to be individually owned, and with a rule that this initial endowment should be respected. Tom might own the fuel and the flour, Dick the ovens and the walnut trees, Harry the spades, and so on. The point of it all being that production requires much more *organisation* than simple trade. If cakes are to be baked and eaten, then a solution has to be found to the problem of who digs and who bakes, what recipes are to be used, how many cakes are to be baked and in what proportion, and who will eat them. Tom, Dick and Harry will have to be prepared to swap and *cooperate*. To bake the maximim number of cakes with their combined resources, they will have to swap their individual endowments, be prepared to participate in joint ventures, and ensure that baking can be continued day after day. With the pattern of ownership in which Tom and Dick had nothing except their labour to offer, enterprising Harry, the owner of all the other means for baking cakes, would make the production decisions and employ the other two to do the work. He would pay them in cake and leave them to trade among themselves if a better cake allocation could be so achieved. A situation in which each man owns sufficient tools and equipment to bake cakes on his own would still leave room for trade if each specialised in making one kind of cake. Even collective ownership of the means of production—Tom, Dick and Harry jointly owning all the ingredients and tools for making cakes—might result in specialised production and trade in ready-baked cakes. Once production has been admitted, the starting point becomes one of an *initial endowment* of physical resources and personal abilities, defined by *property rights*. Individuals then trade among themselves in both the means of production and the goods produced to arrive at the exchange optimum. The pattern of individual ownership and the distribution of personal attributes, as well as individual tastes and appetites, determine the outcome within the rules of the game.

Three men on an island have exhausted their usefulness, their problems of production are too simple, their numbers too small, and the variety of their goods too limited. Nevertheless, they have served to illustrate the basic economic function of markets. Their example should be kept in mind through the rest of this chapter.

ECONOMIC EQUILIBRIUM

The social consequences of economic equilibrium are hidden beneath several layers of theoretical analysis. Even the definition of equilibrium involving just two non-identical individuals is not easy. It is as well, therefore, to begin with the simplest possible example. As explained above, in a pure exchange economy the problems of production can be ignored, and attention focused on trade and consumption. Every individual receives an initial bundle of commodities. The size and composition of the initial bundle are determined arbitrarily according to no obvious rules or pattern, rather in the way the helicopter made drops of individual parcels on the imaginary island. Commodities may be distributed between individuals in any proportion provided first, that the individual bundles always add up to the total available to society as a whole, and second, that inequality in the division of the total never reaches the point where any individual has nothing at all. Everyone must have something to trade with, and there must be no waste. Individuals are then free to keep the commodities in their initial bundle, or to change them by trading with other individuals. At the start of the process commodities are held for trade or consumption, and at the end for consumption only.

Individuals will trade with one another as long as they can realise a mutual advantage. When a bargain is struck commodities are exchanged at an agreed rate: the exchange ratio of the crude barter economy, or the relative price of the sophisticated money economy. With only two consumers each bargain determines both the price and the amounts to be traded. If they agree to trade 1 bicycle for 10 transistor radios the exchange ratio can be deduced as 1 bicycle=10 transistor radios while the relative price becomes 1 bicycle=£60 (or \$120 or Fr 600) and 1 transistor radio=£6 (or \$12 or Fr 60). They do not find the relative price ready-made and then decide how much, if anything, to trade at that price. They may try out different prices before reaching agreement, so they ought not strike a bargain and actually complete the exchange until they are sure no better terms can be extracted from the trading partner. When all the possibilities have been explored and both parties are content—a contentment limited by the situation in which they find themselves—an *equilibrium trade* and an *equilibrium price* have been determined. Neither individual wants to change the bargain because neither can find any advantage in recontracting. The outcome (the final distribution of the commodities available to society between its members) is the product of an initial allocation and voluntary exchange.

There is no guarantee that the two traders will find an equilibrium, nor, if they find one, that it will be the optimum. Poor communications and imperfect knowledge may keep them apart; mutual suspicion and lack of bargaining skills may stop them reaching agreement. Movement away from the original allocation only has to benefit at least one of the traders. So several bargains will be available which give better consumption opportunities, though not necessarily the best to both. The balance of advantage between them will depend in part on their relative bargaining strengths. If the number of traders is increased then there are literally more competitors. One trader can be played off against another, coalitions formed and dissolved, bargains struck and broken. Any final and lasting agreement has a better chance of being the optimum.

In an economy with many commodities there will be many prices; and if all commodities are traded they can be linked together in the familiar pairwise fashion, bicycles with

Markets

transistor radios, transistor radios with cheese, cheese with wine, and so on, until all relative prices are determined. If they are consistent with each other then the whole economy may be said to be in equilibrium. A model with just two traders and two commodities cannot really be used to explain general equilibrium, but its workings can be drawn on two-dimensional diagrams and its simplicities are sufficient to reveal the weakness of the market as an aggregation device.

In Figure 7.1 wine is measured on the horizontal axis and cheese on the vertical axis. The size of the box gives the total amounts of the two commodities available to the society composed of Him and Her. How will the 8 units of wine and the 6 units of cheese be allocated between Him and Her as a result of trade? His wine and cheese is measured from the bottom left-hand corner of the box, so the closer ˉHe approaches the top right-hand corner the better; Her position is exactly the reverse of His. Their interests are mutually exclusive. The only constraint is that they must be

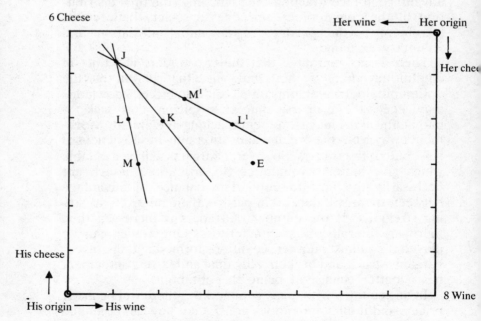

Figure 7.1: Finding a trading equilibrium

somewhere in, or on the edges of, the box, with no unused commodity. At point E, for example, they have equal shares of wine and cheese (4 wine and 3 cheese each).

It would be more realistic, however, to assume that they start with unequal shares. Let them begin at a point such as J, holding before trade;

J:	Him	1 wine	5.3	cheese
	Her	7 wine	0.7	cheese
		8 wine	6.0	cheese

They will only stay put at J if either their respective holdings perfectly match their respective needs, or there is some artificial impediment to trade. Rejecting the first supposition on the grounds that it could only be the result of a lucky accident, and the second on the grounds that the purpose of the exercise is to examine the working of perfect markets, there remains the problem of in which direction and how far they will move. Now although it is true that what one holds the other it is denied, they do not have to enjoy the commodities with the same intensity. Thus it may be possible to find other points in the box which would make them *both* better off, trading wine and cheese between them. The opportunities for trading are represented by the exchange rates of wine and cheese, and the slope of a straight line pivoted through J will measure different relative 'prices'. In a market both traders must agree to pay the same relative price, so the problem is narrowed down to finding a common price at which they will strike a bargain, or actually 'swop' so many units of wine for so many units of cheese.

If the line is pivoted too far to the left, making wine relatively expensive in terms of cheese, He will be faced with potential trades which make Him worse off than at J (note His original holding of wine). Similarly, if the line is pivoted too far to the right, making cheese relatively expensive in terms of wine, She would be prepared to stay at J (note Her original holding of cheese). Putting the situation crudely, He will not want to be pushed nearer to his origin than He is already, and She will not want to be pushed nearer to Hers.

Take the line drawn through points L and M. This relative price is something like 1 unit of wine 'costs' 3.3 units of cheese. He might be prepared to move away from J at this price as far as L, giving up some of His cheese (of which He holds the greater part) in return for a little more wine. Point L represents His preferred trade along the line. Moving further away from J makes Him feel worse off than He would be at L, and moving towards J makes Him feel worse off than He would be at L. She, on the other hand, is prepared to move as far as M, giving up a little of Her wine (of which She holds the greater part) in return for much more cheese. Point M represents Her most preferred trade along the line, in the same sense that L represents His best trade. Several positions on the line might be better for both of them than staying at J, but not as good as L for Him and M for Her: the most preferred positions do not coincide. In the case of the price line drawn through points M^1 and L^1, 1 unit of wine 'costs' something like 0.5 units of cheese. She finds Her most preferred trading position at M^1 and He finds His at L^1. Her holdings of wine are much less valuable, and His holdings of cheese much more valuable. Once again their best trading offers are incompatible.

Only at the relative price shown by the slope of the line drawn through K might a bargain be struck at which both traders can attain their most preferred positions from the initial endowment of J. Here 1 unit of wine 'costs' 1.3 units of cheese, He offers 1.3 units of cheese for 1 unit of wine, and She offers 1 unit of wine for 1.3 units of cheese. Exchange takes place and society moves to a final allocation (trading equilibrium) of:

K:	Him	2 wine	4 cheese
	Her	6 wine	2 cheese
		8 wine	6 cheese

He may not be very happy knowing that She has more of both commodities to consume. Even for Him, nevertheless, the final allocation is an improvement on His initial endowment. Given the choice between J and K, He will always take K. Given the balance of the original endowment, She was bound to obtain the better bargain in also choosing K rather than J. There is no reason to expect points like J and K to be unique: the traders could be placed by an initial endowment anywhere in the box. There is, however, reason to believe that the final trading equilibrium reached from any initial endowment will lie on a locus of such points through K.

One further example is given in Figure 7.2, in which indifference curves are introduced to provide an additional explanation for trader choice. The new initial endowment is at P, and the new trading equilibrium at R. He obtains the better bargain. His indifference curves are labelled Um^1, Um^{11}, Um^{111} to indicate rising levels of ordinally measured utility; Hers are labelled Uw^1, Uw^{11}, Uw^{111} to convey identical information. At initial endowment J He is on indifference curve Um^1 and She on Uw^{11}. There is, of course, no necessary connection or comparison between His or Her levels of utility, but it is clear that neither will be prepared to move in trade to positions on lower indifference curves. So as long as trade puts them inside the area bordered by Um^1 and Uw^{11}, both will be better off. Point K

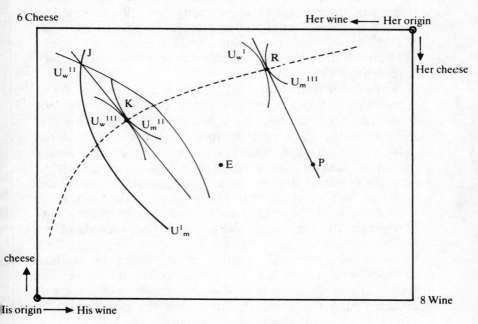

Figure 7.2: Finding the contact curve

is the trading equilibrium because they can both reach the highest of their respective indifference curves (Um^{11} and Uw^{111}) from J at the price measured by the slope of the line JK. It is a point of common tangency between their indifference curves and the price line. Exactly the same conclusions apply to movement from P to R, although only the indifference curves of the final trading equilibrium are drawn. Every time the initial endowment is changed another equilibrium will be found and another point discovered on the dotted line through K and R. Even the equal shares endowment at E will prove unsatisfactory. He prefers cheese to wine, She prefers wine to cheese, and they can strike a mutually advantageous bargain somewhere between K and R. Moreover, this relative preference and trading direction explains the position and general shape of what is called *contract curve*. From anywhere on the diagonal drawn from his to her origin in Figure 7.2, He wants more cheese and She wants more wine. Their indifference curves are of such a shape that the points of common tangency fall above and to the left of the diagonal. If He prefers wine to cheese, and She cheese to wine, the points of common tangency would fall below and to the right because their indifference curves would have different shapes.

While both traders are better off on the contract curve than off it, and each point on it can be described as efficient in the sense that the best use is being made of endowments, there is conflict in movement along the curve. One trader is made worse off as the other is made better off. Efficiency means a neutral matching of commodity allocation to consumer wants. Equity means judgement between the utility or welfare level of different identifiable consumers. Within the world of ordinal utility, and without interpersonal comparisons, there is no way of judging between points on the contract curve other than by pointing to the obvious fact that the interpersonal distribution of utility or welfare changes in favour of one or the other consumer. Nevertheless, it is important to note that the equilibrium price will change along the contract curve with the distribution of utility or welfare even when individual preferences are constant.

TRADE WITH DIFFERENT ENDOWMENTS

The introduction of production pushes back the explanation of final allocations one stage further. No longer do individual members of society start with an apparently free gift of commodities. Commodities must be made before they can be consumed The simplest way of handling the problem is to assume that society has available a fixed amount of productive resources and a certain level of technical knowledge. Its resources are human and non-human, tools and minerals, land and buildings, as well as personal abilities to work and organise. The ownership of the means of production is distributed in some arbitrary fashion among individuals (including their human attributes), and becomes the *initial endowment*. Individuals trade among themselves in the factors of production, selling labour services, renting land, hiring machines, until they have achieved the best possible voluntary production arrangements. As a result of the acts of production individuals have earned 'claims' on commodities which can be exchanged as in the model of pure exchange. Thus there are two kinds of market, a factor market and a commodity market, and the final allocation of commodity depends on bargains struck in both areas. If an individual is lucky enough to be strong and healthy, to possess skills which are scarce and productive, to own large tracts of fertile land or large numbers of technically-advanced machines, then he should emerge in the commodity market in a very strong bargaining position. Whether his potential is realised depends, in the case of human attributes, on his attitudes to work and leisure. A gifted individual may choose to trade only a small portion of his abilities because he prefers a lifestyle combining little work and much leisure to one combining much work and little leisure. Depending upon the total value of his personal endowments, this may imply he chooses a low income or a small claim on consumption commodities. What is clear is that relative preferences between work and leisure become as important as relative preferences between commodities in determining the impact of any initial endowment.

In terms of the two-dimensional diagram used here most

of these choices and trades have to be taken for granted. Changes in total endowments, in the productivity of factors or in personal effort have to be represented by altering the size of the consumption and trading box. When the amount of cheese is increased from whatever source, the box is pushed upwards; when the amount of wine is increased, it is pushed outwards to the right. There is little realism in assuming that each factor produces only one commodity. Individuals are likely, therefore, to approach trading after production with a mixed bundle of commodities as before. He and She are endowed with different amounts of both factors—call them land and labour—and both factors can produce wine and cheese, albeit in different proportions. Even with a given total of land and labour of society, given factor productivities and constant preferences between income and leisure, changing the relative endowment of the individuals means that they can be placed anywhere in the consumption and trading box.

Figure 7.3 shows two (overlapping) alternative production bundles (x and y): 5 wine and 6 cheese (x) and 8 wine and 5 cheese (y). One pre-trading allocation is given for each bundle: point P in x, and point J in y. Other interpersonal endowments of the factors responsible for producing x and y, and their respective trading equilibria, have to be imagined. With Him again preferring cheese to wine, and She wine to cheese, the contract curves will be of the general shape given by the dotted lines drawn through R in x, and through K in y.

The origin for Him stays put in the bottom left-hand corner, and His indifference curves are unchanged regard-less of the size of the box. In other words, an allocation at J means the same amounts of wine and cheese and the same level of utility or welfare to Him in x or y. By contrast, the origin for Her moves with the size of the box. The top right-hand corner moves in space. Consequently, Her indifference map has to be redrawn for x and y. The coordinates of J are 4.25 wine and 1.5 cheese for Her in x, and 7.25 wine and 0.5 cheese in y. There is no reason why they should yield the same utility levels. Indifference curve Um^{11} in x is undoubtedly higher than Um^1 in y, because they

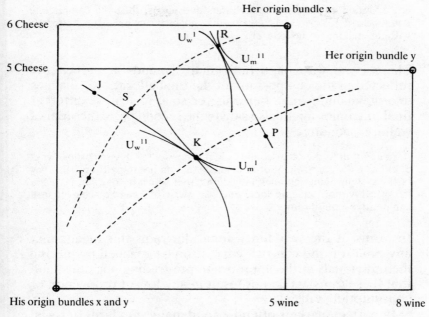

Figure 7.3: Trading with different endowments

are members of the same map. Indifference curve Uw^{11} in y may be higher than Uw^1 in x, or it may be at the same level, or it may even be lower. In this exercise the consumer often ends up with more of one commodity and less of the other, because of endowment and not because of trade.

THE MARKET AND COLLECTIVE RATIONALITY

The equilibria imagined here to be determined in the perfect market economy are the best (the most efficient) outcomes for all participants within the limits set by their endowments. In other words, they satisfy what is called the first basic theorem of welfare economics:

If all participants act competitively, if there are properly functioning markets for all commodities and factors traded, and if there is complete and accurate information about offers and prices, then the competitive equilibria, if it exists, will ensure that no one can be made better-off without making some one else worse off.

There is no waste and individual demands are efficiently reflected in the composition of the final allocation. Changes in original endowments engineered so as to achieve different final outcomes might also satisfy the second basic theorem of welfare economies:

> If, in addition to the other conditions, it is possible to devise costless ways of altering the endowment of individuals that do not impair the efficiency of the system, then any final allocation (from which no one can be made better-off without making some one else worse off) can be achieved as a competitive equilibrium.

In terms of the two-dimensional diagrams this means that any point on the contract curves can be reached by placing the individuals at the appropriate pre-trading positions, and that these *transfers* do not result in any loss of production or consumption efficiency.

Imperfect markets offend a good many standards of social acceptability, including Arrow's own test. The real force of the impossibility theorem, however is directed at the workings of perfect markets. Like first past the post methods of election, they are not designed to generate a social ordering. By amalgamating individual preferences, they simply pick a 'winning' (efficient) social state. Each social state should include a description of the composition of a commodity bundle, its efficient production and consumption. In the realm of consumption it is confined to the allocation of the commodity bundle and an associated common (social) valuation of the commodities in the bundle. Points like K and R in Figures 7.2 and 7.3 represent equilibrium allocations of the bundles in their consumption and trading boxes, and their equilibrium prices measure the relative social valuation. Inconsistency enters the choice process because a different winning allocation of the same bundle of commodities, and a different social valuation can be derived from the same set of individual preferences or tastes. Points like K and R in Figure 7.2, or like R, S, and T in Figure 7.3, are different social states, and each could be chosen by the same choice process from a different initial allocation of the same bundle. The market cannot order or choose between the points on the contract curve for commodity bundle x in Figure 7.3. The individuals whose indifference maps are drawn in Figure 7.3 do not change their preferences between wine and cheese. But when personal economic circumstances change, so will the bids consumers can afford to make for wine and cheese, and so will the allocation the market selects as the winner or the optimim. With the initial endowment at P, the optimal allocations for x will be at R, and R will be socially preferred to S or T, or to any other allocation in the box on or off the contract curve. With other initial endowments the market will just as clearly pick another winner. The paradox is that while the market always selects one of the equilibrium allocations, it cannot really compare them. Individual consumers know that different endowments and allocations bring them different benefits; the market does not know such things. Endowments are externally determined and play no part in its choice. The market records and amalgamates individual bids for commodities anonymously: £5 from a rich man is as little or as much as £1 each from five poor men. Thus the market is irrational in changing its mind for no good reason.

Inequality as such is not the central problem. If endowments were distributed in a very unfair and unequal way between individual members of society, and *remained fixed* for all time in that mould, there would be no collective irrationality from market processes. With the same bundle of commodities, and the same set of individual preferences, the market would always (correctly) choose the same equilibrium allocation and relative price. Individuals may have ethical preferences (judgements about distribution) but the market is not interested. Its very efficiency in information-collection rules out that kind of aggregation.

It must also follow that the market is unable to compare the optimal allocation of different bundles of commodities. In Figure 7.3 T, S and R are candidates for the winning allocation of bundle x, and K is one of the candidates of bundle y. The fact that the market may grind out K in y and R in x, with their associated equilibrium prices, provides no information about the relative social welfare of x or y. Real national, income-type calculations or compensation tests might throw some light on the issue, not markets.

REFERENCES AND READING

Although the analogy between voting and the market is frequently drawn by Arrow, he gives little detail. There is a hint in a footnote on p. 110 of *Social Choice and Individual Values* 2nd edn.

The impossibility of moving from individual preference maps to a social indifference map has been fully explored by P. A. Samuelson, 'Social indifference curves', *Quarterly Journal of Economics* (1956), reprinted in *Collected Scientific Papers of Paul Samuelson*, Vol. 2.

For an alternative view of the market, and of the lack of analogy between individual behaviour in the market and in voting, the reader should begin with F. H. Knight, *The Economic Organisation* and then two path-breaking papers by J. M. Buchanan, 'Social choice, democracy, and free markets', and 'Individual choice in Voting and the market', both in the *Journal of Political Economy* (1954), and reprinted in his *Fiscal Theory and Political Economics: Selected Essays*.

Technical details of markets are helpfully revealed in W. S. Vickrey *Micro-Statistics*, Vivian Walsh, *Introduction to Contempory Microeconomics*, with an essential part of the latter reprinted in Harry Townsend (ed.) *Price Theory*, 2nd ed. They are exhaustively treated in Peter Newman, *Theory of Exchange*.

8 Compensation Tests

Economic policies designed to provide the community with a bigger and better bundle of commodities are almost bound to change the distribution of utility or welfare. In moving the economy from one commodity box to another, in other words, they usually benefit some people and hurt others, and end up at a different point on the contract curve with a different equilibrium price. On those rare occasions when at least one person is made better off and no one worse off, unanimity of opinion should be available to confirm that community welfare had increased: the beneficiaries of the policy will approve and the rest will not oppose. When some people are made better off and others worse off, the Pareto test for an improvement in welfare is not applicable. Even though the losers may be in a minority, there is no proof that their combined welfare decrements are smaller than the combined welfare increments of the majority. Majority voting is not enough. This attitude to economic welfare, as argued in Chapter 6, encourages acceptance of the *status quo*. Compensation tests are an attempt to break out of the impasse. If a policy increases the commodity bundle for community consumption far enough then surely it can be shown, in principle, that the gainers can afford to compensate the losers and still have something left over to enjoy themselves. Hypothetically, the potential losers would be willing, after receiving compensation, to approve, or at least acquiesce in, a policy they previously opposed. Hypothetically, society would be unanimous again.

It is easier to think of compensation as hypothetical if the intention of the policy is to provide a bigger and better bundle of commodities, and not to change distribution. Changes in distribution are incidental. Where the gainers are the poor and the losers are the rich, the incidental effects may also be welcome. Why then bother to compensate the rich? Where the policy provides a new bundle which benefits only the rich, there is always a danger that the incidental

131

effects will become more important than the intentional. Why not then keep the old bundle and redistribute that in favour of the poor? Moreover, the mechanics of payment— the calculation and administration of the necessary transfers between all the gainers and losers—would be an almost insuperable task. For all practical purposes, compensation has to be an imaginary exercise, conducted by external authorities convincing themselves that gains from a policy change collectively exceed the losses. The market will find a new equilibrium when the bundle of commodities is altered. But the market cannot distinguish between the old and the new in terms of social welfare. Ideal markets may ensure efficiency in allocation. They cannot ensure justice or equity. Compensation tests are an extra-market device to check whether an improvement in efficiency will lead, in principle, to and improvement in social welfare. They fail to provide a clear and consistent answer because they lack a complete set of ethical preferences. A sign of their failure is the intersection of utility possibility curves, and it is this ambiguity which underlines the impossibility of the market.

COMPENSATION AND BRIBERY

Imagine a policy change which restricts the import of wine and encourages domestic cheese production. The community will have more cheese and less wine available for internal trade and consumption. Cheese consumers—particularly those who prefer cheese to wine—and those engaged in cheese production are likely to be better off as a result. Wine consumers—particularly those who prefer wine to cheese and those engaged in the wine import business, are likely to be worse off. One test for an improvement in social welfare is to ask whether the gainers could compensate the losers (i.e. make them as well off as they were before the change) and still be better off themselves. If the answer is yes in principle, then the policy is to be recommended.

During the discussions about the proposed policy change (to make any practical sense the hypothetical compensation has to be calculated before the policy is implemented) the potential losers might organise themselves and attempt to bribe the potential gainers into abandoning their support for restrictions on wine imports. If the potential losers could make the potential gains as well off before as they would be after the change, and still be better off themselves in the *status quo* position, then the policy has nothing to recommend it. So a second negative test for an improvement in social welfare is that the losers cannot bribe the gainers. Provided both tests give consistent answers, either compensation can be paid and bribery cannot, or compensation cannot be paid and bribery can, the conclusions are clear. In the first case, social welfare will increase when the policy is implemented, and in the second case it will decline. Inconsistent answers (either compensation and bribery can be paid, or neither compensation nor bribery can be paid) lead to uncertain conclusions. Social welfare might increase, or it might decline.

LUMP-SUM TRANSFERS

How is the compensation or bribery to be calculated? In what units are they to be (hypothetically) paid? There are three methods of altering the final allocation of commodities between consumers, of placing them on different indifference curves, in this simple model. First, and most fundamental, there is the redistribution of property rights, or of the initial endowments in non-human factors of production. (Enlarging and widening opportunities for education and training may help diminish differences in labour productivity, but nothing as yet can be done about inequalities in innate ability or temperament.) Factor markets will find a new equilibrium, and individuals will enter trade with new holdings of purchasing power or claims on resources for consumption. Second, there is the redistribution of income or purchasing power after production and before trade. The results of factor markets are interfered with, and individuals placed in different positions for trade and consumption than their initial endowments of factors, and factor prices would have determined. These new holdings lead to a new equilibrium on the contract curve. Consumers are free to choose how to spend their income, with whom to trade, and what commodities to consume. There is no interference with consumer prices. Third, commodities can be transferred directly between consumers, ignoring the working of both factor and consumption markets. Consumers end up with a bundle of commodities which they might not have chosen.

Notwithstanding the prospect of the least disturbance to the workings of efficient markets, the first method threatens the greatest political and social disturbance. The third method probably offers the most accurate interpersonal reallocation of consumption, but the greatest loss of efficiency and doubtful effects on interpersonal utility levels. For these reasons most exercises with compensation tests assume that transfers are of income or general purchasing power, and that movement of individuals is from one point on the contract curve to another. To avoid interference with market choices, they ought to be in a *lump-sum* form. They ought not to be related, for example, to the number of hours worked, or to the number of units of a commodity purchased. Taxes or bounties on *income* and on *particular expenditures* must not be used to take away so many £s from the cheese consumers and producers and give them to the wine consumers and importers. Instead a poll (head) tax or bounty, if feasible, should be used to shift the potential gainers and losers to a new initial allocation for trading, from whence they can find the new equilibrium in consumption.

In the following imaginary exercises let x stand for the bundle of commodities *before* the policy of restricting wine imports and encouraging domestic production of cheese, and let y stand for the bundle of commodities *after* the policy has been implemented. Assuming that the application of compensation tests can be demonstrated on two-dimensional diagrams, let Him stand for those who gain from the change to y, and let Her stand for those who lose. The distribution of the original x bundle, which makes Her relatively well off is called x_1. The expected distribution of the y bundle, which makes Him relatively well off, is called y_1. Argument about policy, therefore, is confined to a comparison between the x_1 before and the y_1 after. Hypothetical compensation and bribery, to see if social welfare will increase between x_1 and y_1, introduce two more distributions. Compensation of the losers after the change means finding a distribution of the y bundle which makes Her at least as well off as She was before (at x_1), and is called y_2. Bribery of the potential gainers means finding a distribution of the x bundle which makes Him at least as well off as He would be after the change (at y_1), and is called x_2. To get the society of two individuals (hypothetically) from x_1 to x_2, and from y_1 to y_2, lump-sum transfers are required because x_2 is supposed to be on the same contract curve as x_1, and y_2 on the same contract curve as y_1.

COMPENSATION POSSIBLE, BRIBERY IMPOSSIBLE

The case in which the bundle of commodities has grown so much in all directions that both tests signify an increase in social welfare is illustrated in Figure 8.1(a). It must have been the result of a policy which encouraged both wine and cheese production, or of an adventitious improvement in wine and cheese productivity. It serves as a control for the cases in which the tests give different answers, and in which

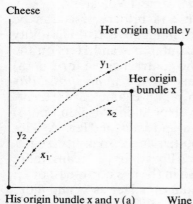

Figure 8.1(a): Compensation tests with consistent answers

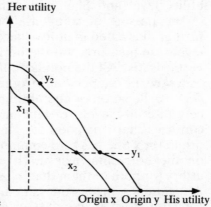

Figure 8.1(b): Non-intersecting utility possibility curves

policy is not so even-handed or generous in outcome. Society moves from x_1 to y_1. His origin is again in the bottom left-hand corner of the box for x and y. Her origin is again in two places depending on the size of the box, but always in the opposite corner to His. She has two indifference maps for the same preferences and He has one. He is much better off at y_1, than at x_1, and She is much worse off. A redistribution of income with the bundle y which moves them down the contract curve to y_2, however, allows Him to compensate Her so that She is no worse off than at x_1 (not on a lower indifference curve) and He is still better off (on a higher indifference curve). If the redistribution had moved them any further towards His origin He would have had no gains left to spare. If the redistribution had fallen short of y_2, She would have been worse off than at x_1. By contrast, She could not bribe Him to stay at x_1. A redistribution of income with the bundle x which moves them along the contract curve towards Her origin fails in the attempt to make Him better off than He would be at y_1. At allocation x_2 She exhausts all her capacity to bribe because any further movement towards Her origin for x would make Her worse off than She would be at y_1. Comparing y_2 directly with x_1 shows that they both enjoy higher utility levels at y_2, whereas comparing x_2 with y_1 shows that He enjoys a lower utility level and She enjoys the same level at x_2.

The passing of compensation and bribery tests can be further illustrated in utility space. In Figure 8.1(b) His utility levels are measured on the horizontal axis and Hers on the vertical axis. All the points on the contract curve for x in (a) can now be mapped into points on the *utility possibility curve*. Allocation or equilibrium y_1, for example, represents certain utility levels for Him and Her and its position in (b) confirms that it is good for Him and bad for Her. At Her origin for x She has zero commodities and zero utility, so it is on the horizontal axis in (b). Allocation y_2 means more utility for both of them than x_1, so in (b) it is north-east of x_1. Allocation y_1 means the same utility for Her as x_2 and more for Him, so it is due east of x_2. A utility possibility curve shows the maximum amount of utility that can be achieved for one consumer at each given level of utility for the other by redistributing its associated bundle of commodities. Maximum utility is shown because all the points are assumed to be efficient in their use of the bundle, derived as they are from the contract curve. Utility is not necessary in cardinal units, however, and the only essential feature is that they fall from left to right, reflecting the conflict of interests between Him and Her. They need not be smooth or have a continuous slope; they need not measure the rate at which one consumer's utility can be substituted for the utility of the other.

The fact that the utility possibility curve for y lies everywhere outside of the curve for x confirms the superiority of bundle y. Wherever the individuals are on the curve for x, there exists a distribution of y which makes at least one of them better off and the other no worse off. Wherever the individuals are on the curve for y, they will be in the north-east quadrant of a point on the curve for x. Compensation will always be possible, bribery never. These conclusions are supported by an analysis of the bundles in terms of individual and social preference. Using the familiar notation:

$$\text{Him:} \quad y_1 P x_2 P y_2 P x_1$$
$$\text{Her:} \quad y_2 P x_1 P y_1 I x_2$$
$$\text{Society:} \quad y_2 P x_1$$

there is unanimity (including acquiesence) in the choice of the y bundle over the x bundle for some distributions. Social choice between the distributions y_1 and y_2 is uncertain because of the direct clash between Him and Her. Reversing the comparison so that society starts at y_1 and considers moving to x_1, with Her as the gainer and Him as the loser, gives consistent answers, only now for staying with bundle y. In reverse, compensation will be impossible, bribery always possible.

COMPENSATION IMPOSSIBLE, BRIBERY IMPOSSIBLE

It is time to reconsider the original example of a policy change which increases one commodity and reduces the other.

Suppose wine is increased and cheese reduced, with the same individual preferences. In Figure 8.2(a) the alternative boxes for x and y are overlapped, and their associated contract curves drawn as in Figure 8.1(a). The difference is that there can be no certainty about the relative positions of x_1 and y_2, and x_2 and y_1. Perhaps He is unable to afford to compensate Her, and She is unable to afford to bribe Him. Failing the compensation test implies that when they have reached point y_2 on the contract curve for bundle y, He has exhausted all His gains enjoyed at y, and She is still worse off than at x_1. In terms of indifference curves, She is on a lower level of utility at y_2 than x_1; and He is on the same level as at x_1. Society should stay at x_1 because there is no evidence of an improvement in social welfare from the move to y'. Failure of the bribery test implies that when they reach x_2 on the contract curve for bundle x, She has exhausted all her advantages of staying at x_1, and He is still worse off than he would be at y_1. He is on a lower utility level and She is on the same level. Society should move to y_1 because there is evidence that x_1 offers lower social welfare. Inconsistent answers mean that the tests can give no clear direction as to the desirability of policy changes in this case.

The same result can be described by intersecting utility-possibility curves. In Figure 8.2(b) redistributing (com-

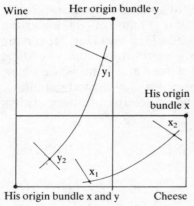

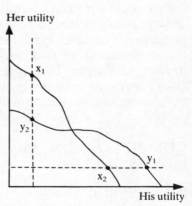

Figure 8.2 (a): Compensation tests with inconsistent answers (I)

Figure 8.2 (b): Interesting utility-possibility curves

pensation) from y_1 to y_2 puts Him back to the utility level of x_1, but leaves Her still worse off. Redistributing (bribery) from x_1 to x_2 puts Her back (or forward) to the utility level of y_1, but leaves Him still worse off. Neither compensation nor bribery makes them both better off, or even makes one better off and the other no worse off. Neither curve lies entirely inside (or outside) the other, so a distribution can always be found which lies in the north-east quadrant of the other. In terms of individual and social preference:

$$\begin{array}{ll} \text{Him:} & y_1 \; Px_2 \; Px_1 \; Iy_2 \\ \text{Her:} & x_1 \; Py_2 \; Py_1 \; Ix_2 \\ \text{Society:} & y_1 \; Px_2 \\ & x_1 \; Py_2 \end{array}$$

There is no unanimity about x and y. On one distributional comparison they agree that x is better, and on another they agree that y is better. Compensation and bribery tests, it should be remembered, are used to derive a social choice between the x bundle and the y bundle, not a social ordering between x_1, y_2, y_1, and x_2.

COMPENSATION POSSIBLE, BRIBERY POSSIBLE

This is not the only kind of inconsistency which the example can generate. It is just as likely that She finds herself on a higher level of utility at y_2 than at x_1 (Figure 8.3(a)). Note the reversion to wine on the horizontal axis, and cheese on the vertical. Compensation may be possible. As the move down the contract curve for bundle y, He can afford to make Her better off than She was at x_1 and still have something in hand himself. Similarly, when they move up the contract curve for the bundle x, She can afford to make him better off than He would be at y_1 and still have something in hand for Herself. He finds himself on a higher level of utility at x_2 than at y_1. Bribery is also possible. Society should move from bundle x to bundle y because there is evidence of an improvement in social welfare. Society should move back again from y to x (or stay at x) because there is evidence that x offers an improvement in social welfare.

The utility-possibility curves again intersect, only now the personal locations have changed. Redistributing (compensation) the y bundle from y_1 to y_2 makes them both better off (Figure 8.3(b)): y_2 is in the north-east quadrant of x_1; but x_2 is also in the north-east quadrant of y_1, so redistribution

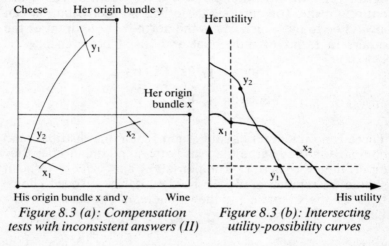

Figure 8.3 (a): Compensation tests with inconsistent answers (II)

Figure 8.3 (b): Intersecting utility-possibility curves

(bribery) of the x bundle from x_1 to x_2 also makes them both better off. In terms of individual and social preference:

$$
\begin{array}{ll}
\text{Him:} & x_2 \; Py_1 \; Py_2 \; Px_1 \\
\text{Her:} & y_2 \; Px_1 \; Px_2 \; Py_1 \\
\text{Society:} & x_2 \; Py_1 \\
& y_2 \; Px_1
\end{array}
$$

There is again no unanimity about x and y. They agree – employing only strong preferences this time—that x_2 is better than y_1, and that y_2 is better than x_1. They cannot give a clear answer to the question, Is social welfare higher with bundle y than with bundle x?

INCONSISTENCY AND IMPOSSIBILITY

Nothing is inevitable about the relative utility or welfare positions of the two individuals in Figures 8.2(a) and 8.3(a).

A policy change which increased the amount of one commodity and reduced the amount of the other might not have led to inconsistency. It might still have produced clear evidence of an improvement in social welfare between bundle x and bundle y. Nor does the construction of intersecting utility-possibility curves, and their associated indifference maps, in itself provide a satisfactory explanation of the failure of the test for hypothetical compensation. It only describes what they must look like. None the less, the combined circumstances of changes in the commodity composition of bundles and changes in interpersonal distribution provide the key. Without them, utility-possibility curves would not intersect.

Changes in commodity composition can have distributional consequences. Individuals with the same income levels can have different utility levels depending on the relative prices of the commodities they want to consume. If the availability of cheese is increased in bundle y compared with bundle x and the availability of wine is decreased, those who prefer cheese to wine will gain and those who prefer wine to cheese will suffer, other things being equal. Cheese will become cheaper in terms of units of wine: i.e. £s of general purchasing power will buy more units of cheese than wine. In all figures He prefers cheese to wine and She prefers wine to cheese, but in Figure 8.2(a) it is wine which is increased and cheese which is decreased. The contract curve, with the same individual preferences and with cheese now on the horizontal axis and wine on the vertical, falls below and to the right of the diagonal between His and Her origins. Wine will become dearer in terms of cheese. On the grounds of commodity composition alone, She is the gainer in the move from x_1 to y_1 in Figure 8.2(a), and He is the gainer in the move from x_1 to y_1 in Figure 8.3(a).

What distinguishes these exercises, however, is that the distribution of income or general purchasing power also changes. In both figures He has more purchasing power at y_1 than at x_1, and She has less. The arguments of Chapter 7 have shown how movements along the contract curve tend to shift the equilibrium relative price of the two commodities. In Figure 8.2(a) movement towards Her origin (from

y_2 to y_1, or from x_1 to x_2) will tilt the relative price in favour of cheese. As His bargaining strength (his command over total resourses) grows compared with Hers, He will be able to exact favourable terms of trade in the commodity he prefers. Commodity composition and income distribution work in opposite directions: the former makes wine cheaper, the latter makes cheese cheaper, and the final outcome is a balance between them. In Figure 8.3(a) distribution still makes cheese cheaper, *and* commodity composition makes cheese cheaper. The two influences work in the same direction. An approximation to the kind of price movements likely to occur are given by the slopes of the lines drawn through the comparison points in both figures.

In terms of levels of utility or welfare, the move from x_1 to y_1 in Figure 8.2(a) means that He loses from commodity composition but gains much more from distribution. She gains from commodity composition but loses much more from distribution. When He tries to compensate her for the net loss, He is unable to find enough £s to make her as well off as She was at x_1 without Himself being worse off than at x_1. When She tries to bribe Him not to take the net gain, She is unable to find enough £s to make Him as well off as He would be at y_1, without making Herself worse off than at y_1. The y box is unfavourable to Him and wine (the commodity She most wants) more expensive at y_2 than it is at x_1. The x box is unfavourable to Her and cheese (the commodity He most wants) more expensive at x_2 than it would be at y_1. Compensation and bribery are impossible. In Figure 8.3(a) He gains in utility levels from commodity composition and distribution. She loses from both. When He tries to compensate her, He finds he has more than enough £s to make Her better off at y_2 than She was at x_1. When She tries to bribe him, She finds she has more than enough £s to make Him better off than He would be at y_1. Bundle y is favourable to Him, and bundle x is favourable to Her. The commodity She most wants (wine) is cheaper at y_2 than it was at x_1, and the commodity He most wants (cheese) is cheaper at x_2 than it would be at y_1. Compensation and bribery are possible.

It is important to remember that individual preferences

remain constant throughout the exercise. The failure of compensation tests to produce unambiguous signals about improvements in social welfare when all feasible distributions are taken into consideration is related to the intersection of utility possibility curves in identical circumstances. But it is the intersections themselves which demonstrate the impossibility of the market. Its neutrality with respect to interpersonal distributions, and the non-uniqueness of competitive equilibria, produce inconsistent social choices.

REFERENCES AND READING

The literature on compensation tests is extensive. The foundations were laid by Hicks, Kalder and Scitorsky: J. R. Hicks, 'The Foundations of Welfare Economics', *Economic Journal* (1939) (available in his *Wealth and Welfare*); N. Kaldor, 'Welfare Propositions and Interpersonal Comparisons of Utility', *Economic Journal* (1939); and Tibor Scitovsky, 'A Note on Welfare Propositions in Economics', *Review of Economic Studies* (1941) (the latter two available, together with the Samuelson article cited in Chapter 2, 'Evaluation of Real National Income', in Arrow and Scitovsky, *Readings in Welfare Economics*). An addendum Hicks wrote in 1981 to his 'The Measurement of Real Income' is useful (Chapter 7 of his *Wealth and Welfare*).

Modern textbook treatments, with references to recent literature, can be found in Yew-Kwang Ng, *Welfare Economics* ch. 3 and Appendix; and E. J. Mishan, *Normative Economics*, Introduction and ch. VII. These two use community indifference curves as well as utility possibility curves, and show how the former can be derived.

The geometry of this chapter owes more to Francis M. Bator, 'The Simple Analytics of Welfare Maximisation', *American Economic Review* (1957), which is also available in W. Breit and Harold Hochman (eds), *Readings in Microeconomics,* and in H. Townsend, *Price Theory* (1st edn ,1971). I. M. D. Little, *Critique of Welfare Economics,* ch. VI should also be consulted, although the arrangement of points for comparison is on a slightly different basis.

9 Utilitarianism

Arrow's approach to social welfare consists of defining reasonable and minimal rules which should govern the derivation of social choice from any pattern of individual values. As both individual values and the social choice are expressed in terms of preference orderings, society's ordering of the alternative social states must be an aggregation of individual orderings. Individuals are assumed to prefer those alternatives which offer them the most utility or welfare and so the social choice will represent the alternative which maximises social welfare, if conflicting individual preferences can reconciled. No formal restrictions are imposed on the nature and range of individual values, nor is any reason given for questioning the fairness or justice of a social outcome provided it has been generated by a process which obeys all the rules. Notions of justice and fairness relate only to the choice of the rules and the respect paid to individual values.

Not everyone is prepared to leave all judgements about social welfare to the soundness (or otherwise) of social choice mechanisms. Four examples will be explored in this chapter, the first three being within what might be called a broad utilitarian framework. Utilitarian assumptions are so deep-seated in the social sciences, and particularly in economics, that it is often difficult to disentangle the deliberate from the accidental or unconscious. Bentham's guiding principle for social acts—the greatest happiness of the greatest number or, to be more accurate, the greatest happiness of all whenever possible, and the sacrifice of a little of the happiness of the few for the greater happiness of the many only when it is not—seems to lead naturally to the idea of maximising social welfare. But the discovery of one overall objective utility against which the consequences of both individual and social acts can be judged, is a mixed blessing. It can produce some very strange and unpleasant results unless constrained by some equally strange assump-

144

tions about the nature of this thing called 'utility' and of the 'individuals' who make up the society in which it is being maximised. For these reasons, the first example chosen is of minimal utilitariamism, a pure economist's notion of welfare maximisation; and the second is of classical utilitarianism with all its strengths and weaknesses.

THE BERGSON - SAMUELSON SOCIAL WELFARE FUNCTION

The social welfare function associated with the names of Bergson and Samuelson has much in common with the way in which Arrow sees the problem of reaching decisions about social welfare. Social welfare is taken to be a function of individual utilities, and each individual utility is to count. Individual utility, in turn, is a function of commodities consumed. Individuals should be free to choose those commodities which they prefer, which maximise their utility. Utility is measurable in ordinal not cardinal units; in numbers which are unique only up to a monotonic transformation, and which cannot in themselves be used to make interpersonal comparisons. Where the Bergson - Samuelson function differs from Arrow is in explicitly excluding feelings of benevolence or malevolence from individual utility functions (they are strictly selfish), and in taking individual values as given (there is no intention of devising a procedure for dealing with every possible pattern of individual values). Bergson and Samuelson imagine a set of externally given interpersonal judgements being imposed upon the outcome of an efficient economic system with given tastes and technology after everything else has been decided, not before.

The productive and allocative efficiency of an economic system has been described in Chapter 7. With a given technology and limited inputs (endowments) in the simplest case, productive efficiency means that there is no way of increasing the output of any one commodity without reducing the output of another. Inputs are being put to their best uses, and there is no waste. The particular combination of commodities to be produced depends upon individuals' preferences. Allocative efficiency means two things: one, that inputs are devoted to the production of commodities which consumers as a group most prefer; and two, that commodities are enjoyed by individual consumers in amounts from which its is impossible to deviate without making one better off (enjoying more utility, having preferences met more fully) at the cost of making another worse off. If it were possible to increase the utility of one consumer by allocating some more commodities to him, without diminishing the utility of another, the system would be wasteful.

This Pareto condition for maximising economic welfare has a severe limitation. There is no unique solution, rather a number of maxima, each satisfying the same requirement for a different distribution of relative welfare. Movement along the contract curve—literally a locus of consumption efficiency points—makes one individual better off and the other worse off. Redrawing the contract curve in terms of utility rather than goods—mapping all the points on the contract curve into utility space—gives a utility possibility curve as in Chapter 8. But just as there is no unique equilibrium for the efficient allocation of a given bundle of commodities, so there is no unique production bundle for a given endowment of factors and technology. Each bundle will present a different allocation problem and generate a different contract curve. The utility possibilities for consumers, as Chapter 8 demonstrated, are a function of the composition of commodity bundles *and* their interpersonal distribution. The same bundle can put the consumers at different points on its contract curve with a different interpersonal utility distribution, and the same interpersonal utility distribution can be found with more than one bundle on more than one contract curve. These are the reasons why utility-possibility curves intersect. A description of the *maximum* opportunities for interpersonal utility is now required.

In Figure 9.1 the line joining points E and F on the axes for His and Her utility represents an outer limit of feasible interpersonal utility distributions, with constant preferences between commodities on the part of the two individuals

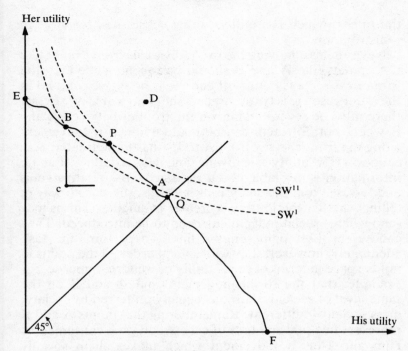

Her utility

E

B

P

D

c

A

Q

SW¹¹

SW¹

45°

His utility

F

EF=Grand utility possibility frontier.

Figure 9.1: Possible Bergson - Samuelson social welfare contours

concerned, and a given production technology. All points within and on the bounds of the whole area OEF are attainable, while all points outside, such as D, are not. As the object of the exercise is to maximise social welfare, attention can be focused on the points between E and F on the outer boundary. Each of them stems from a bundle of efficiently produced and consumed commodities, and each represents the highest levels of combined utility for Him and Her in the sense of pushing them both furthest out towards the north-east for that particular relative utility distribution. But because this so-called *grand utility possibility frontier* is drawn in ordinal utility space, it must also be a line rather than a smoothly-sloped curve. Its general shape indicates that gains to Him must entail losses to Her, and vice versa, without measuring the exact relationship between them or the rate at which His utility can be substituted for Hers in redistribution.

Nevertheless, moving the two individuals from a point like C to points like A and B should be recommended. In the former case She is better off and He is no worse off; and in the latter case He is better off and She is no worse off. In fact there must be several points on the frontier between A and B where both of them can be made better off. Movement along the frontier—say from A to E—has to be treated with caution: Her utility is growing and His is falling, but no information is available about the size of the relative gains and losses. From the analysis as it stands, there is no way of telling whether total utility is greater or smaller. This is why (and where) social judgements need to be introduced. They choose the best point on the line. To perform the task adequately, however, they will have to order all the points in utility space in terms of social utility or welfare. Suppose, for example, that the social judgements put A and B on the same level of social welfare, as equally preferred by society, or as socially indifferent. Remembering that points A and B represent unequal amounts of cheese and wine consumed by Him and Her, a judgement which makes them socially indifferent also indicates how much Her increased consumption at B (compared with what it was at A) is required in compensation for His reduced consumption at B (compared with what it was at A) to keep social welfare constant. The dashed lines superimposed on Figure 9.1 are contours of a hill of social welfare, with the peak somewhere to the north-east. Each contour traces out those combinations of His and Her utilities (derived from His and Her consumptions of cheese and wine) which are judged to be of equal *social* welfare. They are all drawn convex to the origin, sloping away from the two axes, revealing that there are diminishing returns to the social welfare in trade-off between His and Her utility, and that no one is allowed to have zero utility. So as His utility is reduced, more and more of Her increased consumption is required in compensation for His reduced consumption to keep social welfare constant.

On the interpersonal bias of SW^1 and SW^{11}, points A and

B are judged superior to point C and inferior to point D (although that particular contour has been omitted). Point P is superior to both A and B, being on the higher contour SW^{11}, and becomes the best point on the utility-possibility frontier. There is nowhere else on EF where a higher level of social welfare can be reached. It maximises social welfare given the constants of production and consumption. But there is no reason why Bergson - Samuelson contours should have this bias. They could be biased towards Him rather than Her, or they could have an egalitarian bias and select points on the frontier which lie on or near the line of equality (drawn through point Q at 45° to the axes, though in ordinal utility space the actual position must be rather fuzzy). Any asumption is permissible as long as the chosen point lies on the utility-possibility frontier and the contours which effectively make the choice exclude extreme positions. Someone has to formulate these judgements—perhaps an ethical observer who could be any member of the community—but it is not something the economist as pure economist needs to worry about.

SIMPLE UTILITARIANISM

If individual utilities can be measured by a unique set of numbers, across all members of the community, then utilitarians may conduct comparisons of social welfare entirely in terms of the sum of those utilities. If they are prepared to ignore differences in the distribution of utility between individuals, non-utility information about interpersonal relations, and the identity of those who gain and lose, then utilitarians have a powerful and consistent index of social welfare in all possible social states. Simple examples will make the point clear:

Social state:	x	y	z
Her utility:	6	4	4
His utility:	10	12	13
Sum of utilities:	16	16	17

There is no detectable change in social welfare between

social state x and social state y: the increase in inequality, and the fact that it is *She* who loses and *He* who gains, has no impact on the total. There is an improvement in social welfare between x and z despite the increase in inequality, and between y and z, even though all the gains go to Him. Indeed, there would still be a gain in social welfare between y and z if the numbers reflected a situation in which He started to do some unpleasant things to Her. The sum-of-utilities approach is neutral with respect to both the worth or desert of the people who make up the community (Her utility is just as important or unimportant as His) and the kind of social behaviour which the enjoyment of utility might require (social behaviour which would otherwise be condemned).

Defenders of utilitarianism will protest that this description of their doctrine is a travesty. Neither the founder of the school nor his disciples apply the sum-of-utilities test for an improvement in social welfare in such a crude manner. The argument for utility-maximisation is always hedged around with caveats and exceptions; extreme or absurd conclusions are avoided. Fairness demands that these subtleties are given proper attention to allow a fuller and more sympathetic picture of utilitarianism to emerge. Yet exaggeration does have its uses. It underlines the central role—in simple utilitarianism at any rate—of the adding-up problem. It shows how the need for subsidiary argument weakens the power and simplicity of the overriding objective. It offers the opportunity of establishing the implications of a resilient and influential social philosophy step by step.

The first step is to establish a legitimate use of numbers. Where do they come from? Money income serves most frequently as the proxy for utility. But no one wants to claim that there is a direct, one-to-one relationship between money income and utility. Nearly all utilitarians will want to argue that utility eventually increases at a slower rate than money income above subsistence levels, that a doubling of money income does not represent a doubling of utility. So they have to invent a numerical relationship between utility and the objective measure. Someone has to write down utility numbers against the money incomes of every member of society, and that someone looks very much like the (benevolent and paternalistic) utilitarian observer. However, with the overall objective defined in terms of the sum of utilities, only *differences* in individual utility numbers are relevant. It does not matter what the absolute levels of utility are, or in what units they are expressed, as long as the net effect of their changes can be measured. Uniqueness up to a linear transformation would provide enough information. Linear transformations churn out the same answer, keeping the same sign for the net change in the sum of utilities. All the previous numbers could be multiplied by half, and a constant 10 added to produce:

Social states:	x	y	z
Her utility:	13	12	12
His utility:	15	16	16.5
	28	28	28.5

Although the absolute levels of utility look quite different, the ordering of the social states remains as before, with the net increase being a ½ unit instead of a whole unit. Individual gains and losses also bear the same relative significance. Thus a wide range of numerical devices become available, including those derived as will be seen from expected utility calculations. Whether they overcome the problem of interpersonal comparison in which the size of absolute differences counts as well is another matter.

Equality is only desirable under simple utilitarianism with extra or supplementary argument. Comparison of social states by the sum of utilities has to be limited by some explicit concern for the distribution of that sum between individuals in each state. As it stands, maximising total utility may be served as well by inequality as by equality. If a more unequal distribution is associated with a larger sum, so be it. But even describing the distributional aspects of different social states within an explicit utilitarian framework is too much for numbers which are unique only up to a linear transformation. Both description and judgement require a completely unique set of numbers for the utility of all members of society.

Assume in Figure 9.2 that His and Her utility are measured in identical units and on an identical scale. Crude utilitarian social welfare contours can then be drawn as parallel straight lines at 90° to the line of equality. The vertical and horizontal intercepts of each contour will represent equal amounts of utility (OG=OH), and the intersection of each contour with the 45° line will represent that same amount of utility divided equally between Him and Her (point A, etc.). Drawn in cardinal utility space, the frontier can now have a smooth shape with a measurable slope. In Figure 9.2 it has an indentation at Q because of the disincentive effects upon the supply of labour by Him and Her when redistribution is carried too close to complete equality. The maximum point will not be on the 45° line. The actual shape of the EF implies that slightly more total utility

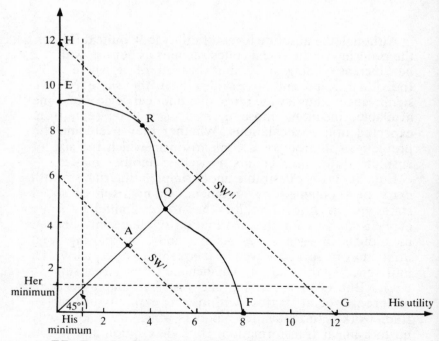

EF= Frontier of feasible utility distributions

Figure 9.2: Crude utilitarian social welfare contours

will be gained by redistribution to Her, and R is chosen by the utilitarian contour SW[11]. Even extreme points like G and H might have been chosen, however, if the frontier bulged out along one of the axes, with one of the individuals having no utility.

Zero options can easily be avoided by insisting that every individual should have at least a minimum level of cheese and wine or of income. His or Her utility would be neither discernible nor measurable until this level was reached. Even then, every conceivable kind of inequality could exist above subsistence. Everything could remain as before between the dotted lines indicating Her minimum and His minimum utility in Figure 9.2. Equality of income is only certain on simple utilitarian assumptions if all individuals are identical in their capacity to obtain utility from income, and it is feasible to redistribute income in any way without loss of output. His and Her utility schedules would have to be mirror-images of each other, as in Figure 9.3. Her income is measured from the left of the horizontal axis, and His from the right. The length of this axis determines the total amount of income available for distribution between them. Equal incomes are at A. Her total utility increases at a diminishing rate from left to right, from zero to all the available income at N. His total utility schedule has exactly the same shape and height, going from right to left with a maximum at M. At B, where the two utility schedules cross, aggregate utility is maximised. Movement away from B to the left or right will reduce the combined totals—one individual enjoying more, the other less—as shown by the aggregate utility schedule MCN (obtained by adding vertically His and Her utility levels) having its highest point C immediately above B. But B lies immediately above A, so maximising total utility requires complete equality in income.

Unfortunately the argument for equality crucially depends on the subsidiary identical 'pleasure machines' assumption. Once it is admitted that some individuals may be better at converting income into utility than others, maximising aggregate utility leads to inequality. If even She, for example, can reach higher levels of utility for the same levels of income than He, then She can claim a bigger share of the total income available. In Figure 9.3 this situation is illustrated by shifting Her utility schedule upwards from ON to ON^1. Vertical additions of the two utility schedules now gives MEN, with a peak in aggregate utility at E immediately above point D on the income axis, representing more

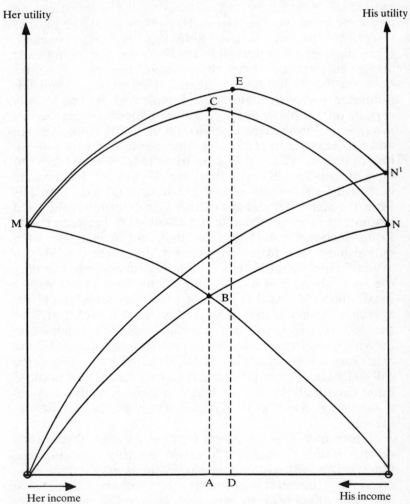

Figure 9.3: Utilitarianism and income distribution

income for Her and less for Him compared to the equal income distribution at point A. The greater the differences in individual powers to convert income into utility, the greater will be the inequalities in income required to maximise aggregate utility. In more realistic (and complicated) examples, when the distribution of the power to convert income utility is not known (is unknowable), no firm conclusions can be reached about the distribution of individual incomes on utilitarian grounds. The only way to retain the completely egalitarian position is to proceed on the assumption that individuals are identical 'pleasure machines'. Imaginary (idealised) individual utility schedules can then be added up as before. Whilst it is pretty obvious that individuals differ in their capacity to enjoy utility from the same commodities, an *as if* assumption does have a certain moral appeal on income distribution. Non-utilitarians might also find it a superior notion about human capacities. But they could take a more direct route to the egalitarian destination by simply rejecting all inequalities in income distribution as morally offensive. They would not even have to imagine any utility aggregation.

For utilitarians, however, there is one other complication (at least). Utility is derived from income, and income is derived from work. Work is unpleasant and yields disutility. Only income and leisure yield positive utility. So maximising utility becomes a matter of balancing the gains from income against the losses from work, and it may have to be quite a delicate act, for there is now the problem that individuals may differ in their power to convert leisure into income, as much as (or even more so than) in their capacities to convert income into utility. It is not just that some people can work harder, rather that they can work more effectively, they are more productive, more able. Nor does there seem to be any compelling moral reason why this particular difference should be assumed away. The most able (the more efficient 'work-machines') should be encouraged to give up more leisure so that everyone can enjoy more income, whether the income so produced is given to all in equal shares, or given mainly to the more efficient 'pleasure machines'. The *sum* of individual utilities will be greater provided the loss on utility suffered by the more able (because they give up leisure) is less than the gain in utility to all who consume the additional income. Thus, in conditions under which everyone has the same utility of income schedule (and the same utility of leisure schedule), social utility will be maximised by equal distributions of income and unequal allocations of work. Obviously great care needs to be taken in the redistribution of income and reallocation of work when these conditions do not hold. If too much of the additional income is given to inefficient 'pleasure machines', and too many of the additional hours to inefficient 'work machines', or if the more able attach higher utility to leisure forgone than the less able attach to income gained, then the sum of utilities may actually decline.

To be successful, social welfare maximisation at this level of sophistication must be based upon accurate and detailed information about all individual utility and productivity functions, and have an effective means of implementing its policies. In a command or centrally-planned economy implementation at least might not be so difficult (the more able would simply be told to work longer), but in a decentralised economy, relying on price signals and incentives, even that may be beyond the government's powers. On the contrary, individuals might have an incentive to ignore the signals and incentives, just as they might want to hide their true productive abilities from both planner and tax collector. Attempts to redistribute income from rich to poor, or to the more efficient 'pleasure machines', can turn out to be counter-productive as far as the sum of utilities is concerned if the tax measures simply lead the more able to work fewer hours (an income tax is a disincentive to work because it lowers the net wage per hour). Many utilitarians have accepted the potential conflict between efficiency and equity and tempered their arguments for equality accordingly, some even to the extent of using the argument for greater equality in the distribution of income only to break ties between social states in which the sum of utilities is the same. But persuading the more able to work longer hours, whilst at the same time taking away part of the fruits of their labour, is the really difficult task. Higher wages are both the incentive and the source of income for the other members of the community. Left to themselves, the more able would maximise their private utilities and work fewer hours than are required by aggregate utility maximisation. They would be better off, society would be worse off. If a tax could be imposed on their *abilities* rather than on their *income,* then higher wages could remain as the incentive, because the additional income they earned could not affect the total tax they paid. By working longer hours they could be better off *after tax*. Regrettably, not only is ability hard to identify and measure, the more able would have every reason to pretend they were stupid, i.e. to hide their true earning potential.

Finally, there is a crude (although quite popular) version of utilitarianism which imparts an egalitarian bias to data about the distribution of income (or of any of the quantifiable index of utility or welfare) in the process of adding up. After all, why should social welfare be a simple sum of individual utilities? Why not take as an example the logarithm of the number of each individual income, and add that up? In this way a certain social weight is attached to the degree of inequality. Suppose the raw data for a community of four individuals took the following alternative forms:

Social state:	*x*		*y*		*z*	
	Income	log	Income	Log	Income	Log
Individual A	10	1.00	25	1.40	10	1.00
B	15	1.18	25	1.40	15	1.18
C	25	1.40	25	1.40	25	1.40
D	50	1.70	25	1.40	70	1.85
	100	5.28	100	5.60	120	5.43

Alternatives x and y have the same total 'income' (or some other index of utility), but in y it is distributed equally among all members of the community. When logarithms are taken, the equal distribution has a higher total. Alternative z is larger than either x or y, but it is distributed even more unequally than is x. When logarithms are taken, z has a lower total than y. Their effect is to place a greater value on equality than inequality, but not to the extent of ignoring the size of the sum altogether. The social utility weight implicitly attached to an income of 10 is 1 (log 10=1.00) and to an income of 100 is 2 (log 100=2); twice the value rather than 10 times the value. Only equi-proportional increases in 'income' give equal *increases* in social welfare:

	A's		B's	
Income	*Log*	*Income*	*Log*
100	2.00	200	2.30
150	2.18	300	2.48
+50	+0.18	+100	+0.18

Both A and B have enjoyed a 50 per cent increase in 'income', so in society's eyes their 'abilities' have increased by the same amount, although the absolute changes in 'income' are very different. More social welfare could be gained by giving the larger (absolute) increase in 'income' to the poor individual (A). Other statistical formulae are available which can give social welfare aggregation every kind of egalitarian twist. The choice of the correct method of adding up individual utilities becomes a matter of balancing the demands of equity (distribution) and efficiency (the sum).

   Simple utilitarianism has sometimes been interpreted to mean maximising *average* utility rather than the sum of utilities. The difference between them reduces to a question of population. Their information requirements are the same: knowledge of at least the changes in the utility levels of all individuals is as necessary for calculating the sign of the change in the average as it is for the sum. But whereas neither interpretation is bound to an egalitarian conclusion, average utility maximisation can lend support to policies which control or even reduce the population when the sum of utility maximisation does the opposite. Suppose the previous example is expanded so that there are four individuals with utility levels of type A, three of type B, two of type C and one of type D. The calculation of the sum and average for this new social state x, with a population of 10 divided into 4 utility classes is:

	Social state x			*Social state y*	
A	4 × 10 =	40	A	8 × 10 =	80
B	3 × 15 =	45	B	6 × 15 =	90
C	2 × 25 =	50	C	4 × 25 =	100
D	1 × 50 =	50	D	2 × 50 =	100

Pop. = 10 Sum = 185   Pop. = 20 Sum = 370
Average = 18.5   Average = 18.5

Average utility will be 18.5 and the sum 185. A doubling of the numbers in each utility class will double the sum but the average stays at 18.5. In social state y the population has doubled to 20 and the sum has also doubled. Average utility will only register an improvement in social welfare if utility increases by more than in proportion to the number of people. Keeping more people alive at the same level is not enough. Keeping fewer people alive at a higher level, however, might be enough if the 'lost' members of the population were from the lower utility class so total utility declined in a smaller proportion. By contrast, sum of utility maximisation would register an improvement in social welfare in the first case, and a decline in the second. Average utility, like total utility, is indifferent to the distribution of any given total of utility between the members of the same population.

REFERENCES AND READING

The Bentham Committee of University College, London is organising a comprehensive study of Bentham's works, and of direct relevance to this chapter are Jeremy Bentham, *Constitutional Code, Vol. 1,* F. Rosen and J. H. Burns; and Frank Rosen, *Jeremy Bentham and Representative Democracy: A Study of the Constitutional Code.* A close companion volume is Ross Harrison, *Bentham.*

Samuelson continues to defend the Bergson-Samuelson social welfare functions in the introduction to the enlarged edition of *Foundations of Economic Analysis*; and in 'Bergsonian Welfare Economics', *Economic Welfare and the Economic of Soviet Socialism*, ed. S. Rosefielde.

Bergson's own position on utility measurement is documented in Abram Bergson, *Essays in Normative Economics;* and *Welfare, Planning and Employment.*

There are now two excellent collections on utilitarianism; Sen and B. Williams (eds), *Utilitarianism and Beyond;* and H. B. Miller and W. H. Williams (eds), *The Limits of Utilitarianism.* Both collections have useful introductions, and the essays by Parthar Dasgusta, Frank Hahn and J. A. Mirrlees in *Utilitarianism and Beyond* are particularly relevant here.

The example of logarithmic addition is taken from D. G. Champernowne, *Distribution of Income Between Persons.* The figure on utilitarianism and equality is derived from Sen, *On Economic Equality;* and Angus Deaton and John Muellbauer, *Economics and Consumer Behaviour* have useful chapters on 'Choice under Uncertainty' and 'Social Welfare and Inequality', with diagrams of social welfare contours.

10 Expected Utility and Maximin

There is nothing new about average utility maximisation. Its virtues and vices have long been recognised. What modern utilitarianism offers, among other things, is a new justification of reaching average (or total utility) policy conclusions. The unravelling of this long and ingenious story involves the notion and measurement of expected utility. In the previous analysis it has been assumed, implicitly if not explicitly, that individuals (and society) are maximising the utility of certain outcomes. When He chooses 6 units of cheese and 4 units of wine He knows that the units will be available, and that He can afford them at guaranteed prices. When She chooses social state x rather than social state y She knows which position, with its attendant privileges and wealth, She will occupy in x and y. One way of dealing with the problem of uncertainty is to assume that individuals maximise the utility of outcomes weighted by their probabilities. The greater the likelihood of an event occuring, given its inherent utility, the greater will be its expected utility. As between two events of equal probability, the one with the greater inherent utility will be preferred. Expected utility maximisation becomes a theory of rational decision-making, an explanation of the determination of preference orderings in the face of uncertainty, and the source of 'utility' numbers on an interval scale.

Imagine an individual faced with two alternative 'lotteries', one a 50-50 chance of becoming either a photographer in Los Angeles (x) or a policeman in London (y), the other a 50-50 chance of becoming either a pastry cook in Paris (w) or a printer in Rome (z). If x were preferred to w, and y to z, then the first lottery would be chosen because, presumably, the expected utility of its outcome exceeds that of the second lottery to the individual. But if the the individual changes his opinions about y and z and favours z over y—while still preferring x to w—and *again* chooses the first lottery, it must indicate that x is preferred to w by more than x is preferred to y. With the same probabilities, the choice of lottery reveals something about the intensity of preferences between alternative occupations. The difference between the utilities of x and w exceeds the difference between the utilities of z and y.

Formally, with L standing for lottery, EU for expected utility and p for probability, this example can be written down as:

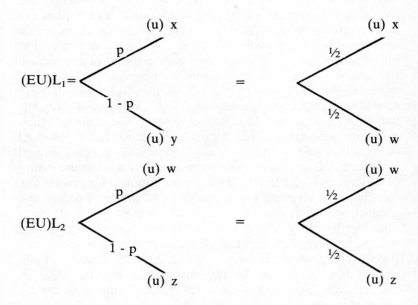

Inferences about utility measurement are derived from a utility theory in the face of uncertainty (usually called the Neumann-Morgenstern Utility Theory) which has the following assumptions or axioms:

(i) Preferences for lotteries are complete and transitive. If L_1 is indifferent to (equally attracted to) L_2, and L_2 indifferent to L_3, then L_1 must be indifferent to L_3.

(ii) Preferences between alternatives are continuous in the sense that, given three ordered alternatives (x P y P z),

there exists some odds between 0 and 1 at which a
lottery combining the most preferred (x) and the least
preferred (z) is indifferent to (equally attracted to) the
intermediate (y) as a certainty.

(iii) Monotonicity, or desire for high probability of success,
which means that, given two lotteries offering identical
prizes the one with the highest probability will be
preferred.

(iv) Independence, or the sure-thing principle, which means
indifference (or any other preference relation) between
lotteries when they differ only in that one offers x and
the other y, and when x is indifferent to y (or any other
preference relation). The presence of a third alternative
should not change preferences between x and y: z
would be an irrelevant alternative. Preferences between
taking a job as a photographer in Los Angeles or a
policeman in London should not be affected by the
chances of being a printer in Rome: taking the job in
Los Angeles rather than the job in London is a sure
thing, if that is how the individual feels about those two
alternatives. Formally,

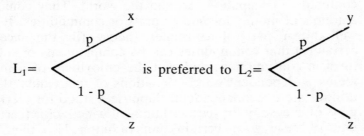

when x P y.

(v) Compound lotteries are treated in the same way as the
probabilities of ordinary lotteries. Preferences between
lotteries which are, in turn, tickets to other lotteries,
should be based upon a calculation of the ultimate odds
offered.

If the axioms are accepted, then it is possible to construct an index for the ordering of lotteries by their expected utilities, which accurately reflects the individuals' actual preferences.

The Neumann-Morgenstern approach is not above criticism either as a descriptive or as a normative theory of individual behaviour. Its axioms have been challenged on logical and empirical grounds. But whether people do treat, or should treat uncertainty in this way is not the issue here. What is of interest is how—conceptually at least—expected utility can be measured in cardinal units whereas most analysis of preferences under conditions of certainty gives rise to utility measured only on an ordinal scale. What makes the difference? Axiom (iv), the independence or sure-thing principle, seems to be the key.

It is important to note that alternative outcomes are treated as mutually exclusive states of the world. Being a photographer in Los Angeles means that you cannot be a policeman in London. The independence assumption also means that the utility derived from x is unaffected, unrelated to the utilities derived from y, w and z, and vice versa. Examples of alternative outcomes, however, cannot be confined to occupations around the world. They could be amounts of money income or units of commodities. It is a well-known part of consumer theory (in the face of certainty) that commodities can be complements or substitutes in consumption, and that the enjoyment of complements is dependent on combinations of their units. Their utilities are not independent. Suppose x stood for (certain) units of cheese, y for (certain) units of wine, w for (certain) units of bread, z for (certain) units of butter. Now there will be no lotteries or probabilities, and individuals must choose between bundles of commodities. Suppose further that one such bundle consisted of 6 units of cheese and 4 units of wine, and another of 5 units of bread and 2 units of butter:

$$B_1 = 6x + 4y$$
$$B_2 = 5w + 2z$$

Even though the individual prefers 6 units of cheese to 5 units of bread (xpw) and 4 units of wine to 2 units of butter (ypz), the first bundle need not be preferred to the second.

The combination of 6x and 4y might yield the same, or even less utility (might be equally attractive or less attractive) than the combination of 5w and 2z, because of complementary effects. Wine and cheese, bread and butter, go together; and the utility from wine and cheese, bread and butter cannot be measured separately and then added together. Bundle 1 might represent an unbalanced combination of wine and cheese for the individual in question. The expected utility approach rules out this kind of interdependence, and inferences can be drawn about the intensity of preferences from choices between lotteries. Thus the way is clear to construct a cardinal index of utility.

EXPECTED UTILITY NUMBERS

In generating a set of numbers to represent preferences between prospects it is necessary to determine a zero and the scale of measurement. Using the example of jobs, the zero point could be the utility of being a policeman in London; and the utility of being a photographer in Los Angeles, a much superior alternative, could be set at 100 units. Although the choice of zero and the subsequent scale is quite arbitrary, once determined they can be used as a standard lottery for computing the utility values of all the other prospects. It simply becomes a question of finding the probabilities of the prospects in the standard lottery which make its expected utility equally attractive to the individual as the third prospect for certain. For example, the certain job of a pastry cook in Paris might be as attractive as the 50-50 chance of being a photographer in Los Angeles or a policeman in London:

$$\text{Utility of w} = 0.5 \text{ (utility of x)} + 0.5 \text{ (utility of y)}$$
$$= 0.5 \ (100) + 0.5 \ (0)$$
$$= 50$$

Given that x is preferred to w, and w to y, the value of z on this scale might be calculated as:

$$\text{Utility z} = 0.4 \text{ (utility of x)} + 0.6 \text{ (utility of y)}$$
$$= 0.4 \ (100) + 0.6 \ (0)$$
$$= 40$$

Once probability and the individual preferences between prospects are known, an index can be determined; any linear transformation of these numbers will provide the same kind of information about utility. Substituting money values for jobs—£ or $ of income instead of being a printer in Rome—makes no difference to the procedure.

Cardinal measurement is of little use in adding up social welfare if interpersonal comparisons cannot be made. Expected utility calculations provide numbers on an interval scale, but they are unique only to the individual being examined. Separate indices could be calculated for every member of society with no necessary connection between them. The scale and origin of every personal index might be different, and—what is more important—any attempt to convert them to a common basis would be open to criticism.

Take two individuals with an ordering of four alternatives:

individual A: zPwPxPy
individual B: xPwPyPz

Assume that separate utility numbers have been determined by expected utility experiments, and that they have then been normalised on a scale marked 0 for the least preferred alternative, 1 for the most preferred, and at proportional intervals in between for the rest:

	Individual A		*Individual B*	
	Original index	Normalised index	Original index	Normalised index
Alternatives:				
y	30	0	150	0.5
x	45	0.5	200	1
w	50	0.67	190	0.9
z	60	1	100	0
	185	2.27	640	2.4

$$\frac{\text{Normalised}}{\text{number}} = \frac{\text{original number} - \text{lowest original number}}{\text{lowest original number}}$$

Whilst the totals of each column look interesting, they have no significance. At this point in the argument the only issue is the fairness of the methods of converting personal numbers (by linear transformation) into normalised numbers. In effect, the conversion table assumes that individuals have the same *maximum* attainable utility: 1 unit. For individual A it is z, and for individual B it is x. Looking across the rows of normalised numbers, alternative w maximises total utility (the fact that the original numbers give that honour to alternative x is irrelevant) alternative x is second, z is third and y is last. Another frequently adopted scheme of normalisation is to make the marks for each alternative add up to 1. In this way it is assumed that every individual enjoys the same *average* utility across the alternatives. Starting from the same original numbers, this linear transformation produces:

Alternative:	*Individual A* Normalised index	*Individual B* Normalised index
y	0.16	0.23
x	0.24	0.31
w	0.27	0.30
z	0.33	0.16
	1.00	1.00

$$\text{Normalised number} = \frac{\text{Original number}}{\text{Sum of original numbers}}$$

Alternatives z and x still yield maximum utility for A and B, respectively, and alternative w the maximim total utility.

Which is the better procedure? Is it fairer to assume equal maximum or equal average utility? Both transformations will preserve the ordering of alternatives and the ratio of differences between the totals, though not the absolute sizes of their differences. In any case, they treat individuals as if they were equal 'pleasure machines'. They ignore the possibility that individuals may differ in their propensity to derive utility from the same endowments of goods, jobs or expectations: one man's numbers may bear no relation to another's. So perhaps there is no correct way of normalising across individual utilities indices, and little point in trying to calculate them in the first place. Perhaps expected utility is an unhelpful digression for social welfare.

Before settling on a pessimistic conclusion about expected utility, the particular requirements of interpersonal comparison need to be explored a little further. It all depends on what is being compared and why. If the *levels* of individual utility are being compared in two social states to determine whether one social state is superior to another, then *units* and *scale* origins are relevant. If social states are being compared by the standard of the *sum* of individual utilities, then the *differences* in utility levels are relevant and the origin of the scale can vary. An example of utility nunbers in interpersonal comparison, in the context of lotteries between alternative projects, brings out the point:

	Prospect x		Prospect y
Lottery 1	$U_A=3$, $U_B=2$	*or*	$U_A=2$, $U_B=3$
Lottery 2	$U_A=3$, $U_B=2$	*or*	$U_A=3$, $U_B=2$

There is nothing to choose between the lotteries as long as the sum of individual utilities remain the test. They both add up to 5 units whether prospect x or y comes about. Yet the distribution of the 'winnings' between the two individuals changes and may form part of another kind of judgement. By the test of levels of utility, however, lottery 2 looks unfair to B because he has no chance of improving on his minimum level (2 units), whereas A has a chance of improvement in both lotteries (up to 3 units). This conclusion requires only ordinal information, examining the numbers to see of B can be better off, not by how much he is better off, nor by how much better off he is than A. As they both have basic minimum level of 2 units of utility, and presumably a common origin for their scales, there is no problem. Unfortunately, if the origin of one of the scales is allowed to move, this information becomes inadequate.

Suppose the origin for B moves so that 1 unit has to be added to all his numbers. His ordering of prospects is undisturbed. Prospect x yields the same number in lottery 1 as lottery 2, the differences between the prospects have identical values, and prospect y has 1 more unit to offer in lottery 2 than in lottery 1. Individual A finds himself as before:

Prospect x   Prospect y

Lottery 1* $U_A=3$, $U_B=3$ *or* $U_A=2$, $U_B=4$

Lottery 2* $U_A=3$, $U_B=3$ *or* $U_A=3$, $U_B=3$

Fairness to individual B is now preserved, and individual A suffers instead. He risks being forced back to the 2-unit level on lottery 1*, whereas B can always do better than 2-units of utility. Distribution has also been given a new twist. Yet by the sum of utilities test there is still nothing to choose between the two lotteries. Individual utilities add up to a larger but identical total. It does not matter who enjoys the units, only that any gain for one individual is exactly offset by a loss to the other. Even when circumstances cause the totals to change, it will be net differences in individual utilities that count, not the original or their scales of measurement.

EXPECTED UTILITY AND SOCIAL CHOICE

Expected utility may have an important role to play in forming judgements about social welfare, although in a less numerate and direct manner. The equi-probability model of moral value judgements, as developed by Vickrey and Harsanyi in particular, applies the concept of expected utility to individuals faced with uncertainty about the particular positions they might occupy in alternative social states. Uncertainty of this kind is supposed to make their values both impartial and sympathetic. They must 'stand outside themselves' and 'place themselves in another's position'. To make comparison in the face of such uncertainty it is no good awarding high utility marks to a social state in which you hope to do well and your enemy badly, because you may have to play the enemy's role. So every position in each alternative social state will be awarded a utility number corresponding to the individual's socially-sensitive assessment, purged of all malevolence and selfishness. Given that the individual has an *equal* chance of occupying any particular position, it is concluded that he will maximise his expected utility by choosing the social state which promises the highest *average* utility. The average or mean of individual utilities in each social state will be equal to the sum of the (expected) utilities from all possible positions divided by the number of (equally probably) possible positions. With equal probabilities, multiplying the utility number of each position by its probability and then adding is equivalent to adding all utilities and dividing by the number of positions. For example, with five possible positions, equal probability is 0.2, and the sum of utility numbers $\div 5 =$ sum of (utility numbers $\times 0.2$).

These thoretical results can be illustrated in the same way as crude average utility maximisation. A example of a population of 10 individuals with the same sum of utility but a quite different distribution as between social states x and y could be:

Expected utility with equal probability

Social state x Individual position utility no:		*Social state y* Individual position utility no:	
A	25	A	5
B	25	B	6
C	25	C	8
D	25	D	11
E	25	E	15
F	25	F	20
G	25	G	25
H	25	H	30
I	25	I	50
J	25	J	80
Sum =	250	Sum =	250

Mean and expected utility=25   Mean and expected utility=25

Faced with an equal choice of being in any of the 10 positions in either social state x or y, the individual should be indifferent. The practical certainty of receiving 25 units of utility in x is balanced by the prospect of doing both much better or much worse in y. Like classical utilitarianism, expected utility maximisation in the equi-probability model seems insensitive to the question of inequality. Larger totals of utility will be chosen in other social states even when they involve greater inequalities. Naturally the outcome would be different if the *objective* chances of occupying individual positions ceased to be equal. Bigger odds on occupying 'the seats of the mighty' would push up the expected utility of social states in which the mighty did very well. The model cannot admit divergences from equi-probability, but it can make allowance for *subjective* feelings towards inequality and risk. Suppose the individual in these imaginary exercises disliked social state y precisely because it involved risk. Preference for the certainty of social state x could be expressed by the award of lower marks to all the individual positions in y. Aversion to inequality could have the same effect. The point is that these feelings are built into the procedure, into the individuals' judgements before the calculation of the average for each social state.

Average utility is clearly the objective to be followed by *individuals* when choosing between alternatives. To say that society can use either average or total utility is at once obvious and problematical. Individuals are not in a position to consider the consequences of changes in population size. Even when 'putting themselves in another's position' their judgement is made from one member of the existing population's point of view, and only the average counts. Society has somehow to reconcile potential conflicts between the two calculations when population grows or declines. But then it should be remembered that the purpose of the equi-probability model of expected utility is to derive a *rule* for social action. Individuals are not actually going to make impartial and sympathetic assessments of every position in each alternative social state, or to calculate expected utilities. The application of utilitarian principles (total or average) at a social level is rather to be justified by the imaginary outcome of individual behaviour in ideal conditions and with the purest of motives. Society should proceed *as if* individuals maximised expected utility and faced the equal probability of occupying any one position in society. More importantly, they are supposed to maximise the same expected utility functions. It is no good imagining each member of society arriving at a differing set of utility numbers. Their capacity to enjoy utility from the circumstances of each person, their psychological make-up, even their attitudes to risk and inequality, have to be sufficiently similar to avoid disagreements about the average utility value of alternative social states. So the 'as if' assumption is about identically moral individuals facing uncertain social outcomes.

MAXIMIN SOCIAL WELFARE

Instead of maximising total or average utility, society could attempt to maximise the utility of its worst off, or least privileged member. A vestige of utilitarianism is retained by the concept of the utility level of the individual, but the measurement is ordinal and there is no attempt to add anything up. Indeed Rawls, the social philospher with whose name this approach to social welfare is now closely associated, would claim that it is deliberately non-utilitarian. Maximin is only part of his theory of justice. Society should arrange the provision of economic and social 'goods'— wealth, income, power, authority—so that the least advantaged member always benefits, and equal opportunities for advancement are open to all. Economic and social inequalities are acceptable when the poor are thereby made better off, not otherwise. Whilst it is true that the principle places an embargo on any move from the *status quo* which makes the least advantaged worse off, policy changes which make everyone better off, including the worse off, are permitted. In utility space the social welfare contours become right-angled, with their corners on the 45° line. Higher levels of equally distributed social welfare shift the contours up the 45° line. Unequal distributions of social welfare are acceptable as long as they lie along one of the arms of each contour, as long as one person is made better off and the other no worse off. Given the utility possibility frontier of Figure 10.1, which is drawn in ordinal utility space like that of Figure 9.1, the best point is one of equality at Q. Like other versions of social welfare, maximin is constrained by

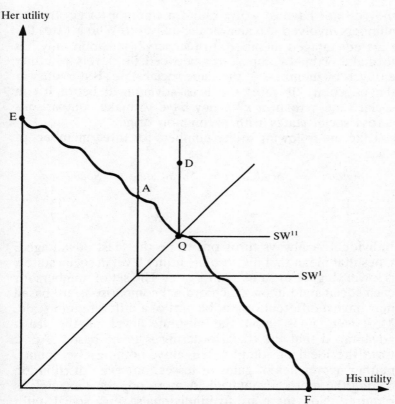

EF = Grand utility possibility frontier.

Figure 10.1: Maximin social welfare contours

the practicalities of redistribution. Like the simple utilitarian version it assumes—in the figure at least—that individuals are identical 'pleasure machines'. Otherwise it would be even more difficult to determine who is the least well off member of society.

So interpretations of the maximin version need to be treated with great care. Levels of utility are one of the key issues. To answer the question, 'Is society as a whole better off in social state y than in x?', utilitarians only have to add up interpersonally comparable differences in utility levels;

they do not have to worry about a common origin for the numbers involved. To answer the question 'Who is (are) the least advantaged member(s) of society?, maximin only has to make ordinal comparisons between the levels of utility enjoyed by members of the same social state. But to answer the question, 'Is (are) the least-advantaged better off in social state y than in x?', they have to make comparisons across social states with a common origin.

Take the following utility numbers for three members of society:

Individual	Social state x	Social state y	Social state z
A	6	4	4
B	10	12	13
C	12	36	107

Individual A always turns out to be the least advantaged. Does that mean that his *absolute* utility level in social state x is lower, higher or same as in y or z? The set of numbers for each social state upon which ordinal comparisons are based may have a different origin, be part of a different unit scale. Moreover, it is upon the absolute level of the least-advantaged that the social ordering is to be based. Apart from the ideal of complete equality, nothing else counts, neither aggregates of gains or losses, nor even distribution among the more advantaged. A more populous example is required. Now there are five individuals, three social states of inequality and one in which every individual enjoys 25 units of utility:

Individuals:	Social state			
	x	y	z	w
A	26	24	24	25
B	28	26	30	25
C	30	26	36	25
D	32	26	40	25
E	34	26	50	25
	150	128	170	125

This information is deliberately over-rich for least-advantaged comparisons. Full unit comparability across individuals and social states shows up its paradoxes. Social state x is superior to the ideal because the least advantaged gains (A has 26 units instead of 25). Social state y is inferior to the ideal (A has 24 units instead of 25), even though everyone else gains and *their* distribution is still equal. There is nothing to choose between social states y and z because the least advantaged enjoys the same level of utility. Close inspection shows that everyone else gains in z compared to y, most of them a great deal, including the next least advantaged (C). By bringing him into consideration the tie can be broken, and z squeezed in ahead of y. Maximin would then be supplemented by *leximin* ((lexicography means dictionary-making, in which words are entered in order of their first letter, and if they have the same first letter, in order of their second letter, and so on, like aard-vark and aard-wolf, hence lexicographic ordering). Application of simple utilitarianism will produce zPxPyPw as a social ordering. Maximin will produce xPwPyIz, and leximin xPwPzPy. (Q and D on the arm of the social welfare contours in Figure 10.1 are no longer indifferent.) The finer points of distribution and redistribution are untouched by these principles. Re-distribution from the middle advantaged to benefit the least advantaged may pass their test, although the distance between the middle advantaged and the most advantaged will have grown wider. As there is no general agreement about how the subtleties of distribution are to be measured, let alone their implications for social welfare, maximin and leximin do not have to face this criticism alone.

Rawls' two principles of equal opportunity and maximin (or the difference principle as it is sometimes called) are part of a wider theory of justice. They simply define its efficiency and welfare aspects. Of greater importance is the system of liberty. Rawls employs the concept of an imaginary social contract, drawn up and agreed by all members of society behind a veil of ignorance so no one knows what actual role they will play in any given society, to arrive at the liberty, the efficiency, and the welfare definitions of the good society'. The first requirement is that everyone shall have an equal right to the most extensive basic liberty (i.e. freedom of speech and assembly, of thought and conscience, to hold personal property, from arbitrary arrest and torture, to vote and hold public office), compatible with a similar right to others. Further, this requirement will be given priority over equal opportunity and maximin. There is no point in worrying about the economic and social welfare of the least advantaged if they (and everyone else) do not possess basic liberties. In choosing between social states, their systems of liberty are examined first, and only when these have been found equally acceptable will their arrangements for the production and distribution of economic and social goods come into account. It is important to remember Rawls' libertarian veto in the application of maximin (and leximin) to particular examples. But what about all the other approaches to social welfare? Ought they not relate to the extent of individual liberty? Should their measurements of welfare and orderings of social states remain unaffected by the erosion of freedoms? Have they got the notion of social welfare the wrong way round by ignoring its most fundamental dimension?

REFERENCES AND READING

Samuelson once more has important things to say in 'Probability, utility and the independence axiom', *Econometrica* (1952), reprinted in *Collected Scientific Papers* Vol. 1. P. Schoemaker, 'The expected utility model' *Journal of Economic Literature* (1982), and Deaton and Muelbauer, *Economics and Consumer Behaviour,* guide and reader through many of the complexities of expected utility and cardinal measurement.

The modern equi-probability approach to social choice is begun by J. C. Harsanyi and W. Vickrey. Harsanyi's 'Cardinal welfare, individualistic ethics, and interpersonal comparison of utility', *Journal of Political Economy* (1955) is collected in his *Essays on Ethics, Social Behaviour and Scientific Explanation.* His 'Morality and the theory of rational behaviour' appears in a special number of *Social Research* (1977), which also contains a useful contribution from Arrow.

Vickrey's 'Utility, strategy and social decision rules', *Quarterly*

Journal of Economics (1960) is reprinted in Phelps (ed.), *Economic Justice*. J. Rawls, *A Theory of Justice* stimulated an important review by Arrow, 'Some ordinalist-utilitarian notes on Rawls theory of justice' in *Journal of Philosophy* (1973) reprinted together with his contribution to the *Social Research* debate in his *Social Choice and Justice.*

Sen has taken a leading part in these arguments and several examples in this chapter have been taken from *Collective Choice and Social Welfare,* ch.9, and *Choice Welfare and Measurement,* essay 9. David Gauthier's 'On the refutation of utilitarianism' in Miller and Williams (eds), *The Limits of Utilitarianism,* has also been used.

11 Liberty and Welfare

The distinction drawn by Rawls between basic and non-basic liberties—and his reward of priority to the first over the second, and to both over social and economic inequalities—is not merely a mark of his concern for justice rather than social welfare; it is also a neat solution to the problems of reconciling utility with non-utility information. Most approaches to social welfare exclude considerations of social life like freedom and justice (and beauty) because they are supposed to be intractable. Freedom and justice do not have a price like material commodities and services, and their relationship to personal utility or welfare is neither simple nor direct. Questions such as, 'How much torture would you be prepared to bear in return for a year's supply of groceries?', sound ridiculous. Questions such as, 'At what level of material well-being does the general right to vote in free elections become significant?', sound too difficult. Yet there is a crucial difference between the first and the second. The first may receive a personal and private answer; the second is designed to produce a social and public answer. While individuals are often forced to make painful choices, and weigh the fairness with which they are treated by the state or other citizens against material advantage, they are not necessarily making value-judgements about what is happening to other people. Freedom and justice (and beauty), therefore, can be included in social welfare assessment as long as they are approached from an individualistic point of view. The gains to those who violate other people's liberty have to be treated on the same basis as the losses to those whose liberty is violated. The profits of those who build ugly buildings are counted together with the disutility of those who have to live in them or look at them. Utility information excludes value-judgements made from a social point of view. Social value-judgements are the intractable part of non-utility information. Suppose there exists a set of fully comparable numbers representing the utility levels of all individuals in all feasible social states. They are dependent upon the economic, political, social and even aesthetic well-being of each individual; the only restriction being that the well-being is personal. If he/she wants, picks, chooses situations in which individual liberties are extensive then that will be reflected in his/her numbers. Similarly, if he impinges on her liberties when exercising his own, that too will be reflected in their respective numbers.

An example of utility numbers for two persons in three social states will be used to illustrate the effect of information restriction. In social state x He has a few material commodities and enjoys 3 units of utility:

Non-utility information ignored: behaviour

Social state:	x	y	z
His utility	3	8	8
Her utility	15	12	12
	18	20	20

She has many material commodities and enjoys 15 units of utility. In social state y She has given him some of Her commodities and the utility difference between them has been narrowed. The total has risen because he gains more utility units as a result of the redistribution than She loses. In social state z He gets drunk every Friday night and hits Her. Although they have the same distribution of goods as in x, He enjoys hitting Her and gains 5 units. She does not like being hit by Him and loses 3 units. So they end up with the same numbers as in y. What is the social ordering? By utilitarianism (maximising the total of utility) and maximining (maximising the utility level of the worst-off individual) y is preferred to x, and z is preferred to x. In the case of z, Him hitting Her is a piece of information about behaviour which is only partly relevant to utility-based orderings. It is important to be clear about the nature of the non-information. His pleasure in hitting Her and Her pain are counted. Society's (other people's) abhorrence of this behaviour is not counted. The point may be brought into sharper focus by taking another, less emotive kind of behaviour. In social state z He now plays loud music on Friday nights which She dislikes. Society may not be as disturbed as it is by violence, although His gain and Her loss from loud music will still be recorded and present the same picture to the utilitarian and maximiner. The implication of ignoring the nature of the behaviour is that people have a right to hit one another, or to play loud music, or to drive dangerously; social welfare is simply a function of individual utilities arising from the behaviour. Behaviour is not the only dimension of well-being to be ignored. Society's view of distance inequality will also be excluded by individual utility numbers. Here is an example of a widening in the utility differences between individuals which is associated with an increase in total utility:

Non-utility information ignored: distance inequality

Social state:	x	y
His utility	3	5
Her utility	15	20
	18	25

Social state y now contains more goods. He has gained 2 units of utility with a few more goods; She has gained 5 units of utility with many more goods. Both the worst-off individual and the community in aggregate are better off. Utilitarians and maximiners would prefer y to x, but society might find the widening gap between members of the community unacceptable. The information from the utility numbers is too rich for those who seek for the largest community total, or the highest level for the worst-off individual. They are not concerned about the differences between levels for any members of the community. By contrast, all the information, and perhaps more, is needed to answer the difficult question, 'Will society's dislike of either behaviour or distance inequality actually reverse the social ordering based on utility numbers?'.

Utilitarianism and maximining are not the only approaches to social welfare which have to try to answer this question. Returning to the utility numbers in the behaviour example, and interpreting them in the spirit of the Arrow rules, would give:

Him: zIyPx
Her: xPyPz

The social ordering would be indifferent between y and z, even though torture existed in z and not in y. Information about behaviour is again irrelevant. Returning to the utility numbers of the inequality example, on similar lines, gives:

Him: yPx
Her: yPx

Society is now unanimously in favour of social state y over x, even though inequality has apparently widened. Information about distance inequality is irrelevant. What each individual prefers, in terms of how the social state affects them personally, is what counts. Moving away from the assumption of pure selfishness will not really help. It is true that individuals may have interdependent utility functions, with one individual preferring (enjoying more utility from) situations in which other individuals are better off, out of feelings of sympathy or benevolence. He may prefer not to hit Her because He feels sorry for Her; She may become disenchanted with the widening gap between Her level of utility and His; and these feelings might be reflected in their personal utility numbers. Unfortunately, interdependence can also be founded on feelings of malevolence. He may particularly enjoy hitting Her; and She may particularly want to distance herself from Him; and this too might be reflected in their personal utility numbers. Rejecting one kind of interdependence, whilst admitting the other would be another example of information restriction. In any case, what society might want to say about violence (or about distance inequality) is not about particular interdependences. Violence would be wrong whether any particular individual(s) liked it or not, and inequality would be limited whether any particular individual(s) found it morally offensive or not. They would be matters of general principle.

The advantages of sticking to individualism, and limiting the number of factors seen to affect welfare, are obvious enough. Value-judgements in the form of general principles based on interpersonal comparisons can be avoided, or at least kept to a minimum. Tractability does facilitate progress towards uncontroversial conclusions about individual and social welfare. But the suspicion must grow that progress has been achieved at too high a price. Some of the things excluded are more significant than those which are included. Of two social states, identical in all utility respects, surely the one which forbids torture, either by private individuals or by agents of the stage, is to be preferred to the one which uses torture as a regular instrument of oppression. The proportion of the population subjected to torture may be small, and the gain to the state (and the pleasure of the torturer) may exceed the pains of the tortured in some crude utility comparison, and still it should be condemned.

For a less emotive example about the dangers of exclusion, consider some of the ways in which individual utility numbers might have arisen. Her relative superiority in distance inequality could have been the result of hard work, ability, inheritance or theft. Hard work and ability might be seen as justifying inequalities in utility; inheritance and theft might not. Thus the same outcome in utility numbers, the same end-state, might have had two contrasting explanations, and might deserve two equally contrasting social values. Most approaches to social welfare, in other words, assess the *consequences* of social organisation and activity and not the underlying causes of that outcome; they are interested in the end-state not the starting point from or the route by which it was reached. Once again the real difficulty lies in trying to reconcile non-utility information with a social or ordering based upon utility information. Is it a matter of degree, balancing the good news of the one against the bad news of the other, or must the introduction of non-utility information make a nonsense of social ordering? Perhaps the whole notion of social welfare is the wrong way of thinking about the goodness and badness of social states.

THE IMPOSSIBILITY OF PARETIAN LIBERTY

Individual liberty means, among other things, that people can do what they please within their private spheres of action, where what they do has no direct, harmful or obvious effects on other people. Translated into the language of ordering, individuals are allowed to be decisive over these private matters and their preferences then automatically become society's preference. Thus if person A wants to travel abroad on his holidays, and in social state x he travels abroad while in social state y—which is identical in all other respects—he stays at home, his preference for x over y must be accepted by society. Liberty has been defined as a situation in which every person has at least one pair of alternative social states, differing only in a private respect, over which he is decisive.

Consider a two-person community faced with three social states which differe only in the matter of travel abroad. In social state x person A travels abroad, and person B stays at home. In social state y B travels abroad and A stays at home. In social state z they both stay at home. It seems reasonable to allow each person to be decisive over the pair of alternatives which affect them personally (whether *they* travel abroad or stay at home) so person A is decisive for society over x and z, and person B on y and z. The liberty (L) condition is satisfied if the social ordering follows their respective orderings over those pairs. It also seems reasonable to conclude that if all members of a community are unanimous in their preferences on any pair, society should adopt their preferences. This satisfies the familiar Paretian condition (P) for reaching a social ordering. Finally, and perhaps not so reasonably, individual orderings can take any combination or pattern. Unrestricted domain (U) is to be satisfied here as it was in the other instances of social ordering. Putting these arguments together means that the society's ordering of the social states x, y and z must satisfy the U, P and L conditions. Suppose now that person A believes travel abroad to be subversive, and further believes person B to have a mind peculiarly susceptible to undesirable foreign influences. Person B, by contrast, believes foreign travel to be broadening, and further believes person A's mind to be especially in need of broadening. Their individual preferences might then take the form:

Person A: zPxPy
Person B: xPyPz

Person A would prefer there not to be any foreign travel, but if there is to be some he would prefer to go himself rather than person B, because it would be less dangerous to society. Person B puts no foreign travel as his worst outcome, but would prefer person A to go first because that would bring most benefit to society. They both seem to worry about what happens to the other more than they worry about what happens to themselves. Their interference or meddlesomeness is not exactly selfless, and has a devastating effect on the consistency of the social ordering. Society's ordering must follow the rules:

xPy   by P
yPz   by L
zPx (and not xPz) by L
xPy . . .

There is a cycle of preference, or intransitivity, between the preference determined by the Paretian condition and those determined by liberty. Given unrestricted domain, there is no way of avoiding the contradiction. It is another illustration of impossibility.

This demonstration of impossibility might be criticised on the grounds that it gives away too much and too little. It gives away too much by allowing *every* member of the community to be decisive over at least one pair of alternatives. It gives away too little by concentrating on a *partial* analysis of feasible outcomes. To meet the first criticism liberty can be redefined to mean that at least *two* members of the community are made decisive over a pair of alternatives in their private spheres: minimal liberty (ML). Enlarging the analysis of outcomes to cover all permutations of a three-sided issue can go some way to answer the second criticism. Instead of an issue of travelling abroad or staying at home, let there be an issue of reading any book, or reading from a censored list of books, or reading only the Bible. Now the outcomes will include (at least) two members of the community doing the same thing as well as doing different things; and each member will have to order every alternative social state describing their doing the same thing of different things. If they both assumed to prefer reading any book, to reading from the censored list, to reading only the Bible, then it becomes convenient to mark these reading alternatives 3, 2 and 1, respectively—numbers indicating a ranking and nothing more. The three sides of the reading issue can thus be distinguished and all the feasible outcomes described in the following matrix:

		Person B		
		Any book	Censored list	The Bible
	Any book	(3, 3)	x (3, 2)	(3, 1)
Person A	*Censored list*	z (2, 3)	(2, 2)	y (2, 1)
	The Bible	(1, 3)	w (1, 2)	(1, 1)

There are nine feasible outcomes which each person has to order. The first number in each bracket indicates what person A is reading, and the second number what person B is reading. (Along the first row person A is always reading any book, down the first column person B is always reading any book, along the second row person A is reading from the censored list, and so on.). The three brackets in the diagonal from top left to bottom right represent those outcomes in which their reading is identical. In all the other brackets their reading is different. For simplicity's sake some outcomes will have to be eliminated. Three go on the grounds that they do not illustrate interference or meddling: the identical outcomes of (3, 3), (2, 2) and (1, 1). Two more go on the grounds that they represent polar outcomes: (3, 1) and (1, 3). Just four are left, identified as w, x, y and z on the matrix. Outcomes (3, 2) and (2, 3), (2, 1) and (1, 2) are combinations of reading any book or the books on the censored list and of reading from the censored list or the Bible.

Minimum liberty now requires each (of the two persons) to be made decisive over one pair of alternatives.

Reason suggests x (3, 2) and w (1, 2) for person A because
reading anything or only the Bible is the decision which
affects *him most dramatically;* and similarly z (2, 3) and y (2,
1) for person B. Whatever affects all the other members of
the community most dramatically does not matter; they
need not be decisive over any pair of alternatives. Unrestricted domain requires that even the following pattern of
individual preferences has to be accommodated:

    Person A: z (2, 3) P w (1, 2) P x (3, 2) P y (2, 1)
    Person B: x (3, 2) P y (2, 1) P z (2, 3) P w (1, 2)

Each person not puts the interests of the other above his
own. The meddling is benevolent. Person A prefers B to
reading anything (enjoying his private first preference), and
himself to read from the censored list, to B reading from the
censored list (B's second preference), and himself only
reading the Bible. Person B's ordering is the mirror-image of
A's. It seems admirable. But it plays havoc with the social
ordering when combined with the Paretian condition. A and
B are like two gentlemen who come to a narrow doorway at
the same time and insist on giving way to each other. If
neither accepts the other's benevolence by relenting on his
own, neither gets through the doorway. An examination of
the individual orderings reveals another social preference
cycle,

xPy		by P
yPz		by ML
zPw		by P
wPx	(not xPw)	by ML
xPy . . .		

There is no way of reconciling U, ML and P. The alteration
of feelings of sympathy into those of hate, so each person
prefers hurting the other to pleasing himself, changes the
individual orderings but not the impossibility result. Person
A would then have yPxPwPz and B, wPzPyPx. With A and
B being decisive on the same pairs as before, society would
emerge with xPwPzPyPxPw . . . as its preference cycle. As in
the case of sympathy, application of the Paretian condition
assumes that every other member of society is indifferent
between all the outcomes which affect A and B. But unlike

the example of travel, in which the meddling was confined to the unanimous pairs, reading has meddling in the decisive or liberty pairs as well. Person B is decisive over y and z, and prefers y (2, 1) to z (2, 3) in the sympathy case, because he prefers to keep as close as possible to person A when the latter is reading from the censored list, to suffer with him. With hate person B's ordering over the decisive pair is reversed: z (2, 3) is preferred to y (2,1) because B can thereby distance himself from A and enjoy A's relative deprivation. Person A's feelings, as well as his preferences, are a mirror-image of person B's.

THE PROBLEM OF INTERDEPENDENCE

Meddling and interference in other people's affairs is a common human failing. The relation does not have to be reciprocal, as in the examples of travel and reading, nor does it have to be motivated by malice or benevolence. One person can impose (confer) a loss (gain) of utility on another quite unintentionally. The response may be to imitate or differentiate oneself from the other's behaviour rather than to try to change the other's behaviour. If person B travels abroad, person A may insist on following him out of admiration or out of desperation to be seen behaving in the same fashion as superior person B. On the other hand, if person B stays at home, A may insist on travelling abroad out of contrariness or out of desperation to be seen not behaving in the same fashion as inferior person B. The decisiveness would seem to lie with B, whether *he* should stay at home or travel abroad. Person A can then respond. As long as the relationship is one-way, and as long as B does not notice (does not mind) whether A follows him or not, there can still be a consistent outcome. But if the relationship works both ways and in opposite directions, so that A wants to differentiate himself from B while B wants to imitate A, the outcome will be indeterminate. Like the two gentlemen at a narrow doorway, they may be paralysed by their interdependence. The example of limitation and differentiation touches on two aspects of personal and social choice which have a wider significance. First, there is *contingency*. Just as A cannot decide on his holiday plans until he knows what B is going to do because he wants to follow him, so A cannot decide on what reading he prefers for himself until he knows what reading B is allowed, because he is more concerned with B's welfare than his own. Secondly, there is the distinction between *freedom* of choice and the *exercise* of that freedom. It is not enough for A to know that B can stay at home or travel abroad; he needs to know whether he is actually going to stay at home or travel abroad. Similarly, A's noseyness with regard to B's reading habits may not be satisfied by knowing that B is free to choose his reading; he wants him to make (wants to stop him making) a particular choice. There is no longer a private sphere of action within which people can do what they please without regard to anyone else. In the two-person, three-alternative illustration of the impossibility of Paretian liberty, *separation of* one person's exercise of his liberties from everyone else's is relatively straightforward. The notion of the private sphere can be rescued by making each person decisive over at least one pair of alternatives, independently of the remaining preference orderings. Drawing up a matrix for staying at home or travelling abroad gives:

		Person B	
		Travels abroad	Stays at home
Person A	Travels abroad		x
	Stays at home:	y	z

Person A determines the choice over x and z, the vertical column of the matrix, and person B the choice over y and z, the horizontal row of the matrix, Thus A would prefer to stay at home and B to travel abroad. Society need not concern itself about any inconsistency between these decisions, nor about the fact that they both prefer x to y. Where A and B take their holidays is an entirely private and separate matter. Indeed society should not be interested in the choices that A and B make in their private spheres. True libertarians ought to say, 'Everybody has the right to travel abroad or stay at home on their holidays, and I should accept their choice whatever it may be, and however much it upsets me.' Yet, in the examples, it is the exercise of choice that counts, not the opportunity of choice. Interference and meddling, imitating and differentiating, depend upon the actual situations in which people have placed themselves, or been placed by others. Even in this simple illustration the descriptions of the alternative social states implicitly postulate a situation for each member of society. With travelling abroad being awarded 2 points, and staying at home 1 point (to distinguish them from each other rather than to predetermine the superiority of travelling abroad) the travel example has similarities with the matrix for reading:

		Person B	
		Travels abroad	*Stays at home*
Person A	*Travels abroad:*		x (2, 1)
	Stays at home:	y (1, 2)	z (1, 1)

Each person is allowed to be decisive over the pair which affects them most directly; person A over x and z because that will decide whether he travels abroad or stays at home, and person B over y and z because that will decide whether he travels abroad or stays at home. To be more precise, A is decisive over his part of the difference between x and z, the (2,-) and the (1,-) elements, and B is decisive over the (-,2) and the -,1) elements of his pair.

Complete separation seems to mean that the individual should ignore the other person(s) aspect of his decisive pair, as well as his wish to influence the other's choice situation. In the holiday example, A's preference for staying at home and B's for travelling abroad are based on their own private preferences. Whether there is a social state in which both can be satisfied is quite another matter. One which merely establishes the right to choose would be admirable. With full weight being given to a minimum libertarian position, and the Paretian unanimity principle being ignored, separation works. In the reading example, by contrast, separation does not work. Person A, it will be remembered, is decisive over x (3, 2) and w (1, 2), and person B is decisive over z (2, 3) and y (2, 1). Their ordering of these pairs, wPx and yPz, respectively, cannot be explained by looking at their personal elements. Given that both individuals are assumed to prefer the widest possible reading for themselves. these elements would require them to order x (3,-) P w (1,-) and z (-, 3) P y (-, 1) respectively. Their preference ordering contradicts purely private interests because it too is contaminated by contingency. Neither of them can make up their minds about the best (reading) social state for themselves without postulating a (reading) social state for the other. A social state in which everyone can make up their own minds what to read will not help. There really are no purely private preferences left. The outcome would be as indeterminate as that arising from individuals who want to imitate or differentiate themselves from each other. A true libertarian solution—at least in the private sphere— is made untenable by the nature of the interdependence each person is assumed to enjoy (suffer).

THE CONFLICT BETWEEN LIBERTY AND WELFARE

What of the alternative to the private sphere? How are these conflicts resolved in the public sphere? For there certainly is a fundamental conflict between those who hold that preferences, judgements and choices about alternative social states—defined in the broadest possible way to include all economic, political and social 'goods' and 'bads'—should be based on the welfare consequences for individuals, and those who hold that the extent and nature of freedom and justice in each state should be giving overriding importance. When individual liberties are universally recognised and treated as unalienable, it does appear that the libertarian interpretation has won over the welfarist. Positive liberties, such as the right to vote in free elections or the right to worship, ignore and override any residual interdependence. The results of free elections are supposed to be accepted by everyone, including the losers. No one is supposed to sell their votes, and no one is supposed to buy them, however strongly they might feel about the harmful effects of other people's voting intentions. Negative liberties, such as the right to be protected against physical violence or arbitrary arrest, are similarly exclusive. The pleasure that some people might obtain from taking part in acts of violence, or even watching acts of violence, is not supposed to count. Once the right has been publicly recognised, the welfare consequences of its exercise and protection are irrelevant. If acts of violence against the person were permitted (placed in the private sphere) then an immediate conflict between unanimity and individual decisiveness could arise. Impossibility is avoided by placing the negative right in the public sphere. Positive liberties in the private sphere, where individuals may express opinions about the way in which each other votes or worships, *and* expect these to be somehow taken into account, will be equally open to the threat of impossibility.

Thus a solution to the impossibility results obtained with the holiday and reading examples could be obtained by making them universal and by placing them in the public sphere. In a sense that is what complete results obtained with the holiday and reading examples could be obtained by making them universal and by placing them in the public sphere. In a sense that is what complete separation implies: choosing where to go on holiday or what to read, without regard to what anyone else thinks or does, is giving liberty public recognition. It is just too bad if some people lose out because they would prefer others to have chosen differently. Social states which grant these kinds of freedom are better than those which deny them. But how extensively should this solution be applied? Is it sensible or expedient to make more than a narrow range of individual liberties universal and public? The argument has some affinities with the distinction between basic and non-basic value-judgements. A basic value-judgement is defined as one which is held to regardless of circumstances. Everyone, for example, has the right to travel abroad on their holidays, even if their response triggers a balance of payments crisis, or spreads a dangerous disease. Again, everyone has the right to read what they choose, even if one book teaches them how to make bombs or hate their neighbours. Many apparently basic value-judgements become non-basic when

tested against particular (and realistic) circumstances. Very
few fundamental individual liberties escape partial amendment. Travel abroad if you like as long as it does not spread
a dangerous disease; read what you like except books which
incite racial hatred. The scope of the exclusions are, of
course, as contentious as the definition of those liberties
which fall properly in the private sphere. There is, however,
another aspect of the distinction; whether the liberties are
alienable or unalienable. A voluntary transfer of rights may
be admissible for those in the private sphere, and not for
those in the public sphere. Votes are not for sale, but the use
of a wide range of property rights, and even the exercise of
rights of personal behaviour, may be voluntarily transferred
or suspended on a reciprocal basis.

Interdependence between utility functions is a familiar
problem to economists. They describe the utility gains
and losses to others from individual private acts
as *externalities*. The way in which people dress,
behave at football matches, spend their income, play
their radios, what they watch on television, and
whether they smoke at home, are all instances of behaviour
which can confer (impose) benefits (costs) on others.
Economists have tried to limit the impact of such external
effects on social welfare by excluding those for which the
sufferer, (beneficiary) is not prepared to 'pay' the actor to
contract (expand). Person A may heartily dislike person B's
hairstyle, eating habits or neglect of his garden, but unless A
is prepared to bribe B to change his behaviour, the
externalities are ignored. Aside from the implications for
distribution and differences in ability to pay, this may be a
reasonable approach to interdependence in the private
sphere. After all, these acts involve the exercise of individual liberties: freedom to behave as you please. Person A
does not have a right to quietness, so if he wants to persuade
his neighbour B to turn the volume of his radio down,
person A must take the initiative and attempt the bribery.
Person A has an implicit right to dress as he pleases and
person B has no right to interfere, so B must try to persuade
A to alter his appearance voluntarily. A solution of trading
in rights is suggested. Person A agrees to amend his

appearance, tone down the colour of his hair, in return for
B's agreement to play his radio at a lower volume after 11
p.m. Person A agrees to stay at home for his holidays in
return for B's agreement to read from a wide selection of
literature. If neither is prepared to offer terms, then the
externality is irrelevant to social welfare. If they are both
prepared to offer terms and cannot reach agreement, or are
not prepared to offer terms because they regard their rights
as unalienable, then the externalities remain and social
welfare—seen as a function of individual utilities—will
suffer. One important obstacle in the way of voluntary
agreements is the often imperfect or incomplete definition of
rights, in particular of ownership rights in things which must
be shared, like quietness and clean air. They cannot be
enjoyed and owned separately, and without separate
ownership there can be neither private bargaining over
individual rights nor the public recognition of individual
rights. Collective decisiveness and collective or joint ownership mean, almost by definition, that some individual
interests are overruled.

The conflict between liberty and social welfare is
about the proper basis for social choice between alternative
social states. Liberty can be regarded as being good
in itself. Social state x is preferred to social state y
because it contains more liberty and not because it contains
more social welfare. Totals of goods and services available in
each state, their distribution between the members of each
state, and the extent to which they meet the needs of those
members, are irrelevant. Indeed, it is possible to extend the
domain of individual liberties to include all the major
aspects of economic life. Rights of ownership in property
and personal labour, together with the voluntary exchange
of those rights and the sale of personal labour, determine the
amount of income each member of society has to spend. *If*
the initial allocation of property rights is itself just and good,
there is freedom in the choice of occupation, in the spending
of income and in the use of leisure (under which might be
subsumed things like reading and travelling abroad), and a
fair system of exchange, then any outcome in terms of
consumption and distribution becomes acceptable. Prefer-

ences between social states depend upon the goodness, justice and fairness of the conditions under which they operate, or the positions from which they start, and not on the positions at which they end. On the other hand, liberty may still be looked upon as part of the welfare of society, as part of the good society, and the consequences of end-states still held in need of correction. It is very difficult to prove to everyone's satisfaction that the initial allocation of property rights was just and good, and if it was not just and good, that its consequences cannot be corrected. Individual liberties may be important, may be given priority, but only as contraints within which social welfare can be maximised. There is a subtle and important difference between saying that social state x is better than social state y because individuals have more liberty in x then in y, and saying that x is better than y because individuals have more liberty in x than in y and *that means x has more social welfare, is a better society*. With the latter statement, when the two social states have the same extent of individual liberty, x's more equal distribution of income can be used to argue that it has more social welfare than y, is a better society than y, is to be preferred to y.

REFERENCES AND READING

Sen has pioneered the work on the impossibility of Paretian liberty (or liberal Paretianism, or Paretian libertarianism) with 'The Impossibility of a Paretian Liberal', *Journal of Political Economics* (1970), 'Liberty, Unanimity and Rights', *Economica* (1976), and 'Personal Utilities and Public Judgements or What's Wrong with Welfare Economics', *Economic Journal* (1979), all reprinted in his *Choice, Welfare, and Measurement*. Two recent papers of his are also of direct relevance. 'Information Analysis of Moral Principles', in Ross Harrison (ed.), *Rational Action*, and 'Liberty and Social Choice', *Journal of Philosophy* (1983). The second of these has been used extensively in this chapter.

Sen gives copious references to his critics and to other contributors to the literature, but two papers have been found particularly helpful, M. J. Farrel, 'Liberalism'. *Review of Econo-*

mic Studies (1976); and Isaac Levi, 'Liberty and Welfare', in *Utilitarianism and Beyond.*

For those who wish to press on with the political philosophy, a good way to begin is with H. L. A. Hart, 'Are there any Natural Rights?' and Sir Isaiah Berlin, 'Two Concepts of Liberty', in Anthony Quinton (ed.), *Political Philosophy.* Alan Ryan (ed.), *The Idea of Freedom,* continues the argument. Robert Nozick, *Anarchy, State and Utopia* offers a provocative and serious attack upon both utilitarian and Rawlsian positions.

Bibiliography

This is a list of books which either have been mentioned in one of the reading and references sections at the end of chapters or are to be recommended for further exploration of the topics raised.

Ackerman, B.A., *Social Justice in the Liberal State* (London and New Haven: Yale University Press, 1980)

Allen, R.G.D., *An Introduction to National Income Accounts and Statistics* (London: Macmillan, 1980)

Arrow, K.J. and Scitovsky, T. (eds), *Readings in Welfare Economics* (London: Allen and Unwin, 1969)

Arrow, K.J., *Social Choice and Individual Values* (2nd edn London and New Haven: Yale University Press, 1963)

———*Social Choice and Justice* (Oxford: Blackwell, 1984)

Barry, B., *Socialists, Economists, and Democracy* (London and Toronto: Collier-Macmillan, 1970)

———*The Liberal Theory of Justice* (Oxford: Clarendon, 1973)

Baumol, W.J., *Economic Theory and Operations Analysis* (4th edn London: Prentice-Hall, 1977)

Bayles, J. (ed.), *Contemporary Utilitarianism* (New York: Anchor Books, 1968)

Bell, D. Kristol, I. (eds), *The Crisis in Economic Theory* (New York: Basic Books, 1981)

Bentham, J., *Constitutional Code* (eds Rosen and Burns, Oxford: Clarendon, 1983)

Bergson, A., *Essays in Normative Economics* (Cambridge, Mass.: Harvard University Press, 1966)

———*Welfare, Planning and Employment* (Cambridge, Mass.: MIT Press, 1982)

Berlin, I., *Four Essays on Liberty* (Oxford University Press, 1969)

Birnbaum, P., Lively, J. and Parry, G. (eds), *Democracy, Consensus, and Social Contract* (London and Beverly Hills: Sage, 1978)

Bishir, J.W. and Drewes, D.W., *Mathematics in the Behavioral and Social Sciences* (New York: Harcourt Brace, 1970)

Black, D., *The Theory of Committees and Elections* (Cambridge: Cambridge University Press, 1963)

Boadway, R. and Bruce, N.,*Welfare Economics* (Oxford: Blackwell, 1983)

Brams, S., *Paradoxes in Politics* (New York: Free Press, 1976)

Breit, W. and Hochman, H. (eds), *Readings in Microeconomics* (New York: Holt, Rinehart and Winston 1968)

Buchanan, J.M. and Tullock, G., *The Calculus of Consent* (Ann Arbour: University of Michigan Press, 1965)

Buchanan, J.M., *Fiscal Theory and Political Economics* (Chapel Hill: University of N. Carolina Press, 1960)

———*The Limits of Liberty* (Chicago: Chicago University Press, 1975)

———*Political Economy 1957-1982* (Washington DC: AEI, 1983)

Champernown, D.G., *Distribution of Income Between Persons* (Cambridge: Cambridge University Press, 1973)

Citrine Lord *ABC of Chairmanship* (ed. Norman Citrine, London: NCLC Publishing, 1952)

Daniels, N. (ed), *Reading Rawls* (Oxford: Blackwell, 1975)

Deaton, A. and Muellbauer, J., *Economics of Consumer Behaviour* (Cambridge: Cambridge University Press, 1980)

Downs, A., *An Economic Theory of Democracy* (New York: Harper & Row, 1957)

Dummett, M., *Voting Procedures* (Oxford: Oxford University Press, 1984)

Farquharson, R., *Theory of Voting* (Oxford: Blackwell, 1969)

Feldman, A.M., *Welfare Economics and Social Choice Theory* (Boston: Martinus Nijhoff, 1980)

Fishburn, P.C., *The Theory of Social Choice* (Princeton: Princeton University Press, 1973)

Frey, B.S., *Modern Political Economy* (London: Martin Robertson, 1978)

Friedman, M., *Price Theory* (rev. edn. Chicago: Aldine, 1962)

———*Capitalism and Freedom,* (Chicago; Chicago University Press, 1962)

Frohlich, N. and Opeenheimer, J.A., *Modern Political Economy* (Eaglewood Cliffs N.J.: Prentice Hall, 1978)

Graaf, J.V., *Theoretical Welfare Economics* (Cambridge: Cambridge University Press, 1957)

Hacker, P.M.S, and Raz J. (eds), *Law, Morality and Society* (Oxford: Clarendon 1977)

Hahn F. and Hollis M. (eds), *Philosophy and Economic Theory* (Oxford: Oxford University Press, 1979)

Harrison, R., *Rational Action* (Cambridge: Cambridge University Press, 1979)

———*Bentham,* (London: Routledge & Kegan Paul 1983)

Harsanyi, J.C., *Essays on Social Behaviour and Scientific Explan-*

ation (Dordrecht, Boston and London: Reidel, 1976)

Hart, H.L.A., *Essays on Bentham* (Oxford: Clarendon, 1982)

Hayek F., *Individualism and Economic Order* (London: Routledge & Paul, 1949)

——*The Constitution of Liberty* (London: Routledge & Paul, 1960)

——*Law Legislation and Liberty, Vol. 2, The Mirage of Social Justice* London: Routledge & Kegan Paul, 1976)

Herman, V. and Mendel, F., *Parliaments of the World* (London: Macmillan, 1976)

Hicks, J.R., *The Social Framework* (Oxford: Clarendon, 1971)

——*Wealth and Welfare* (Oxford: Blackwell, 1981)

——*Classic and Moderns* (Oxford: Blackwell, 1983)

Hodges, W., *Logic* (London: Penguin, 1977)

Holden, B., *The Nature of Democracy* (London: Nelson, 1974)

Hook, S., (ed.), *Human Values and Economic Policy* (New York: New York University Press, 1964)

Kac, M. and Ulam, S., *Mathematics and Logic* (New York and London: Praeger, 1968)

Kelly, J.S., *Arrow Impossibility Theorems* (New York: Academic Press, 1978)

Knight, F.H., *The Ethics of Competition* (New York and London: Harper, 1935)

——*The Economic Organisation* (New York: A.M. Kelly, 1951)

Krupp, S., (ed.), *The Structure of Economic Science* (Eaglewood Cliffs NJ: Prentice-Hall, 1966)

Laslett P. and Runciman, W.G. (eds), *Philosophy, Politics and Society* (Series I, II and III Oxford: Blackwell, 1969)

Little, I.M.D., *A Critique of Welfare Economics* (2nd edn Oxford: Oxford University Press 1957)

Lyons, D., *Forms and Limits of Utilitarianism* (Oxford: Oxford University Press, 1965)

Mackay, A.F., *Arrow's Theorem* (New Haven: Yale University Press, 1980)

Majumdar, T., *The Measurement of Utility* (London: Macmillan, 1958)

Maranell, G.M., *Scaling: A Source Book for behavioural Scientists* (Chicago: Aldine, 1979)

Marshall, A., *Principles of Economics* (8th edn London: Macmillan, 1959)

McGinnis, R., *Mathematical Foundations of Social Analysis* (Indianapolis: Bobbs-Merrill, 1965)

Meade, J.E., *The Just Economy* (London: Allen and Unwin, 1976)

Mellor, D.H. (ed.) *Science, Belief and Behaviour* Cambridge: Cambridge University Press, 1980)

Miller H. and Williams, W. (eds) *The Limits of Utilitarianism* (Minneapolis: Minnesota University Press, 1982)

Mishan, E., *Introduction to Normative Economics* (New York and Oxford: Oxford University Press, 1981)

Mueller, D., *Public Choice* (Cambridge: Cambridge University Press, 1979

Murakami, Y., *Logic and Social Choice* (London: Routledge & Kegan Paul, 1968)

Narveson, J., *Morality and Utility* (Baltimore: Johns Hopkins University Press, 1976)

Newman, P., *The Theory of Exchange* (Eaglewood Cliffs N.J.: Prentice-Hall, 1965)

Ng, Y-K., *Welfare Economics* (London: Macmillan, 1979)

Nozick, R., *Anarchy, State and Utopia* (Oxford: Blackwell, 1974)

Olson, M., *The Logic of Collective Action* (Cambridge, Mass.: Harvard University Press, 1971)

Page A (ed.), *Utility Theory: A Book of Readings* (New York: Wiley, 1969)

Pattanaik, P.K., *Voting and Collective Choice* (Cambridge: Cambridge University Press, 1971)

Pattanaik, P.K., and Salles, M. (eds), *Social Choice and Welfare* (Amsterdam: North Holland, 1983)

Paul, J., Paul, E.F. and Miller, F.D. (eds), *Human Rights* (Oxford: Blackwell, 1984)

Phelps, E., (ed.), *Economic Justice* (London: Penguin, 1973

Pigou, A.C., *The Economics of Welfare* (4th edn London: MacMillan, 1960)

Pitt, J.C. (ed.), *Philosophy in Economics* (Dordrecht: Reidl, 1980)

Quinton, A. (ed.), *Political Philosophy* (Oxford: Oxford University Press, 1967)

Rae, D., *The Political Consequences of Electoral Laws* (New Haven: Yale University Press, 1971)

(with others) *Equalities,* (Cambridge, Mass. and London: Harvard University Press, 1981)

Raphael, D.D., *Moral Philosophy (Oxford: Oxford University Press, 1981)*

Rawls, J., *A Theory of Justice* (Oxford: Oxford University Press, 1972)

Riker, W. H. and Ordeshook P.C., *An Introduction to Positive Political Theory* (Englewood Cliffs NJ: Prentice-Hall, 1973)

Riker, W.H., *Liberalism Against Populism* (San Francisco: Freeman, 1982)

Roberts, B. and Schulze D. L., *Modern Mathematics and Economic Analysis* (New York: Norton, 1973)

Robertson, D. H., *Utility and All That* (London: Allen and Unwin, 1952)

Rosen, F., *Jeremy Bentham: A Study of the Constitutional Code* (Oxford: Clarendon, 1983)

Rosenburg, A., *Micro-economic Laws: A Philosophic Analysis* (Pittsburgh: Pittsburgh University Press, 1976)

Rosefielde, S. (ed.) *Economic Welfare and the Economics of Soviet Socialism* (London and New York: Cambridge University, Press 1981)

Rothenberg, J., *The Measurement of Social Welfare* (Englewood Cliffs NJ: Prentice-Hall, 1961)

Ryan, A., *The Idea of Freedom* (Oxford: Oxford University Press, 1979)

Samuelson, P.A. *Foundations of Economic Analysis* (Enlarged edn. Cambridge Mass: Harvard University Press, 1983)

——*Economics* (11th edn. New York: McGraw Hill, 1979)

——*Collected Scientific Papers* (Vol. 1 & 2 ed. Stiglitz, Vol. 3 ed. Merton, Vol. 4 ed. Nagatani & Crowley, Cambridge Mass.; MIT Press, 1966, 1972 and 1977)

Sen, A.K. & Williams, B. (eds.), *Utilitarianism and Beyond* (Cambridge: Cambridge University 1982)

——*Collective Choice and Social Welfare* (Edinburgh & San Francisco: Oliver & Boyd, Holden Day, 1970)

——*On Economic Inequality* (Oxford: Clarendon 1973)

——*Choice, Welfare and Measurement* (Oxford: Blackwell, 1982)

Simons, H.C., *Personal Income Taxation* (Chicago: Chicago University Press, 1938)

Smart, J. & Williams, B. (eds) *Utilitarianism: For and Against* (Cambridge: Cambridge University Press, 1973)

Straffin, P.D. *Topics in the Theory of Voting* (Boston: UMAP Monograph, Birkhauser, 1980

Sugden, R., *The Political Economy of Public Choice* (Oxford: Martin Robertson, 1981)

Townsend, H., *Price Theory* (2nd edn London: Penguin, 1980)

Tullock, G., *Towards a Mathematics of Politics* (Ann Arbor: Michigan University Press, 1967)

——*Private Wants, Public Means* (Scranton Pa.: Basic Books, 1970)

Vickrey, W.S., *Microstatics* (New York: Harcourt Brace, 1964)

Walsh, V.C., Introduction to Contemporary Microeconomics (New York: McGraw-Hill, 1970)

Index